A Theology for Radical Politics

A Theology
for Radical Politics

Michael Novak

Herder and Herder

1969
HERDER AND HERDER NEW YORK
232 Madison Avenue, New York, N.Y. 10016

My thanks are due to the following publishers for permission to quote from the works cited: Random House for *The Rebel* and *The Myth of Sisyphus* by Albert Camus; Beacon Press for *The New Student Left: An Anthology*, by M. Cohen and D. Hale, eds.; Marc-Laird Publications for *It's Happening: A Portrait of the Youth Scene Today*, by J. L. Simmons and B. Winograd; and the New American Library for *A Prophetic Minority*, by Jack Newfield.

Library of Congress Catalog Card Number: 69–17073
© 1969 by Michael Novak
Manufactured in the United States

Contents

For Gretchen
not a hippie
but 4-H
and still revolutionary

Introduction

The Revolution of 1976

"Each generation has a right to choose for itself the form of government it believes the most promotive of its own happiness. . . . A generation holds all the rights and powers their predecessors once held and may change their laws and institutions to suit themselves."

Thomas Jefferson*

The American Revolution, Thomas Jefferson hoped, would be renewed every twenty years. We have disappointed that hope. When Americans think about revolution, nowadays, they tend to think backwards, *nostalgically—to a crippled man and a bandaged man marching to music of long ago. Have not American patriots in the last ten years tried to rekindle our ideals by turning primarily to memory, rather than to future risks that we must take? To speak of a revolution in the United States is to make many Americans uncomfortable. It seems to many unsettling, subversive, un-American.*

Why do we need a revolution in America? Because the goals to which our people are committed are goals which do not ever entitle us to announce: "This is it. No farther. We have arrived. No more revolutions." The goals to which our people

* Quoted by John Dewey, *Freedom and Culture* (New York, 1963), pp. 157–158.

9

are committed—liberty and justice for all—are goals which require continual self-transcendence, continual going beyond where we are at present. The United States is not now a free society or a just society, nor will it be such a society fifteen years from now, or fifty years from now. To be a free man is an achievement much aspired towards; it is an achievement never wholly attained. The more clearly one knows the meaning of the word and the more sharply one tastes the reality— then all the more powerfully does one realize how far in the future freedom is. We are not free men. We are only trying to become free.

Those who speak too easily of freedom do not deserve respect. We are all guilty of what Sartre calls "bad faith." We say one thing, when we mean another. We claim to be free, then picture ourselves as helpless. "I would like to help you," we say, "but, you see, it's impossible." Or: "I hate to do this; if it were up to me, I would not do it; but the rules . . ." Or: "No man loves peace more than I do. I don't want war. But I'm helpless. It's up to the other side . . ." There is at present enough knowledge and enough money in the world to insure that no human being needs to starve to death. Yet every minute, while we sit here, persons do starve to death. "We are helpless," say Americans. "There is nothing we can do about it."

Perhaps we could begin by being truthful: the truth is that helplessness is the most often voiced sentiment of university people, of politicians, of businessmen, of Americans in general. We are not so much the free world, as the helpless world. We are the not-yet-free people. "We want to do differently. Our heart is in the right place." No doubt the American heart is big enough to try to save the whole world (even if we have to destroy it). "Our heart is in the right place. But we are helpless."

The revolution that is required in the United States is, then, a revolution in the quality of human life, a revolution in the *quotient of human freedom realized by each of us. To too large an extent, freedom in the United States reduces to a consumer's freedom: we are free to prefer Ban to Right Guard, to drive an Oldsmobile rather than a Buick, to work for IBM rather than GM. Politically, we exercise very little control over our city government, our state government, or the policies of our president. We vote for president once every four years, but in between elections it is supremely difficult to have one's counsels listened to, genuinely listened to, even if not accepted. It is possible to feel quite alienated from the American political system, to feel as if our system simply rolls along under its own momentum, to feel as though elections are basically a sham whereby the same policies are executed by the same persons, who merely change faces and names. A growing number of young people feel such alienation.*

What is the role of the university in the coming American revolution? An Israeli friend of mine, who is something of a Marxist, points out that it is an American myth that one can revolutionize a society by making changes in the school system. No school system, he argues, is stronger than the culture in which it lives. By the time students come to the university, they have already been indoctrinated into the dominant values of their society. Moreover, the pressures of the surrounding, all-encompassing society govern the life of the school. Such pressures, in fact, come to be called "reality," and becoming adjusted to them comes to be called "maturity." If you wish a revolution, he concludes, do not waste time trying to change the schools; change the dominant institutions of society, and the schools will change on their own.

In this perspective, the university is almost irrelevant to the coming revolution. The university is a place to which one comes for information, technical skills, and further immersion in the dominant values already existent in one's own society. The university is not a place for learning how to revolutionize one's society. It is a place for learning how to succeed in one's

11

society—it promises a bigger and better career. The university is a training center for good citizens: for talented, capable, happy Americans. "Keep America great. Support your local university."

We must agree, I think, that the Marxist interpretation of the university and the typical American interpretation agree in this most important respect: both assert that the university is basically a tool of the community for inculcating its own basic values. Marxists predict that American universities will produce exactly what typical Americans desire them to produce: typical Americans. American universities will produce trained, skillful personnel able to take their place in the American system. Since, typically, Americans have a mystique about youth, students are expected to be less responsible and more exuberant than their elders—panty raids and protest marches are allowed—but they should not go to "extremes." (In that case, the police will be called.) University officials are expected to temper youthful exuberance with the harsh realities of adult "responsibility." The taxpayers pay for the schools, and so taxpayers have a right, a majority of Americans seem to say, to see that law and order are maintained—their law and order, their society, their established values.

The typical American point of view, manifested in recent polls and in many editorials, articles, and comments, appears to be that a young man is responsible if and only if he conforms to the basic norms, standards, and procedures of our society; that is, if and only if he is not a revolutionary. To say of a student that he is "irresponsible," "far out," "extremist," or even "controversial" is not, in most American contexts, to be recommending him, exactly, for a job. One could conceive of a society, however, which so valued a critique of its own social, economic, and political practices that those who failed to develop revolutionary perspectives would be considered deadwood, conformists, drones, bores, and failures. (In some societies, such students get A's—and that makes the meaning of *"honor student" problematic. For what is the student honored? A student suspicious of the honors passed out by society and critical of himself may deserve to be honored. But then he will be the very one to whom such honors mean least.*)

The American university, in brief, is ambivalent regarding the American revolutionary tradition. On the one hand, a major poll a few years ago revealed that a majority of Americans would, if asked, vote down the Bill of Rights. On the other hand, Americans feel guilty when accused of injustice, inequality of opportunity, or racism. At first they try to deny the facts; they admit the validity of the principle. (Americans could say, for example, "Of course, we're a racist country, and as long as whites remain a majority, that's the way it's going to be. It's to our advantage. Why not?") Thus Americans both commit themselves to revolutionary principles and show little interest in carrying them out. Lots of principle, very little interest: poor banking practice.

A second ambivalence relates to education. Americans want their children to be educated to freedom, but at the same time they want them, basically, to be happy with America the way it is: don't ask too many questions, don't upset the present law and order, don't try to rearrange the bases of power. In short: be free but not revolutionary. The major task of the American way of life is to keep on repeating to people that they are free, while teaching them to be utterly docile. The chief means for doing this is the system of rewards. The more you accept the assumptions of the system (the more, for example, you accept the principle of competition), the more likely your advancement will be. Moreover, the easiest way to end complaints about the system is to raise people's salary by a thousand dollars or so a year. It is not necessary to use a Gestapo to attain conformity; one may just as easily attain it by paying good rewards. In place of bread and circuses, modern technology pacifies our people with cars and color television.

The third ambivalence regarding freedom is a peculiarly

liberal ambivalence. Liberalism as a movement springs from the Enlightenment; it wedded technology to the autonomous individual. But these two spouses are incompatible. The more extensive technology becomes, the less autonomy the individual has. Almost all of us wear wrist watches to synchronize our movements with those of the system of which we are a part. Before we have a chance to protect ourselves, television and radio and newspapers and magazines and books fill our minds and hearts with images and impressions. What falls within that mainstream may be simply asserted, without proof —for example, that the North Vietnamese are "aggressors" in South Vietnam. Whatever falls outside that mainstream must be proved—e.g., that the North Vietnamese are not aggressors in South Vietnam. Statements voiced sincerely by the President of the United States not only must be taken as true until proven false; they also establish a universe of discourse that throws the entire burden of proof upon the dissenters. In brief, technology has put into the hands of administrators a power never before equaled in history. Some philosophers and historians have even been led to say that technology has rendered revolutions in a highly organized society impossible.

Thus many of the most liberal thinkers of our recent history manifest an ambivalence toward freedom of which they seem hardly conscious. They go on using the catchwords of John Stuart Mill, and of their anti-Nazi, anti-Communist, anti-Joseph McCarthy days, as if these catchwords sufficed to deal with the threats to freedom in our time. They do not recognize that the power of the mass media, a competitive economic system, and the politics of ever larger masses of people constitute a far graver threat to our freedom than any faced in preceding eras of our culture. Liberalism sufficed to bring us through World War II. But the managerial, administrative society of the future will use liberals as gears use oil: reasonable, pragmatic, procedurally conscious men who will reduce friction in the system.

14

What, then, does the revolution of 1976—the two-hundredth anniversary of the American Revolution—demand of our universities? Above all, it seems to me, the concept of education as primarily metanoia—*education as conversion. The coming revolution will be moral or not at all. It aims at being a revolution in the quality of American life, a revolution of consciousness. Consequently, its tasks are many. For the first conversion required is a turning to the central question: Who am I? Who? Who? Who? In this brilliant sunshine, under these trees, beneath evening breezes, Who am I? How am I related to my world? But the second question is perhaps even more difficult; it is a question only beginning to emerge with urgency in our century; it arises from the sudden recognition that the question "Who am I?" requires a further question: "Under what institutions do I live?" For before I begin to be responsible for my own identity, I am already being shaped by family, church, economic order, political institutions, school system, mass media, and the rest. Two conversions are required then: one to personal consciousness, and a second to social and political consciousness. "Who am I?" means, in part, "In what kind of society do I live?"*

And the subject who can ask those questions is already condemned to freedom. For he may or may not approve of who he presently is, or what his society is like. Self-knowledge is not only self-discovery (passive)—but self-invention (active, creative). We choose *who we wish to be. The major role of a university, I would suggest, is to establish a community in which those condemned to freedom—every man—must face the risks of freedom. The university often does not at present operate as such a community. To that extent, it inhibits man's growth in freedom, it teaches him to postpone and to evade the urgency of freedom. It brings upon him that greatest tragedy of all: to reach the moment of death in the stabbing realization: "I did not live my own life at all! It was all laid out before me by circumstance."*

15

How do we reintroduce freedom into an industrial, technological state? That is what the revolution of 1976 is all about. Will you help? . . . Will you at least join in the hope that, by 1976, not all of us will be dead in foreign wars, not all of us dead already in life driving in our sleek mobile coffins where alone we seem able to allay our restlessness; and that some of us will still be steadily pursuing that endless voyage of discovery and invention, ever re-creating who we are and what our great nation is?

1. The Inadequacies of the Old Order

I want to bring a radical Christian theology to the support of the student movement of the present generation. The key realities which concern this "New Left" are authenticity, a new sense of community, and a revolutionary employment of power. These realities are of fundamental importance to a Christian. Put more sharply still: it becomes increasingly difficult to see how a Christian can live in these United States and not protest with every fiber of his being against the militarization of American life, the appalling mediocrity of American imagination and sensibilities, and the heedlessness and irrationality of merely technical progress. Moreover, a Christian theologian cannot remain silent at the way in which business and government have industrialized and thus enslaved the university. What is at stake is the quality of human life. When the spirit of man is suppressed, God begins to die. If we may paraphrase Nietzsche: What are these cloverleafs, these napalm factories, these university-industrial complexes, these selective service regulations, if they are not the tomb and sepulchre of man?

1.

The quest for human values in our society, one must say at the beginning, has been radically secularized. It has moved outside the churches. If one wishes to be radically religious in our society—that is to say, radically committed to a vision

17

of human brotherhood, personal integrity, openness to the future, justice, and peace—one will not, commonly, seek an ecclesiastical outlet for one's energies. One will, instead, find community under secular auspices, create one's own symbols for community and integrity, and work through secular agencies for social and political reforms. The saints of the present (and perhaps of the future) are no longer ecclesiastics or churchgoers or even, necessarily, believers in God. The saints of the present are, in the words of Albert Camus, secular saints.

It is a rewarding task to figure out why this has happened and how it has happened. I have tried to treat the issues in *Belief and Unbelief*[1] and in some of the chapters of *A Time to Build*.[2] The main point for our present purposes is that "atheist," "agnostic," or "secular" no longer mean (if they ever did) "nihilist." Dostoevsky has feared that atheism would mean nihilism: "If there is no God, everything is permitted." But his fears have not been realized. In America, atheists retain the chief moral imperatives of Judaism and Christianity; they even become the most serious and imaginative leaders in the attempt to realize these values in our society. Judaism and Christianity have succeeded so well in commending basic human values that perhaps churches are no longer necessary. In the childhood of our culture, they instructed us; in our adulthood, we are on our own.

The other side of this issue, however, is that the chief problems in our society have once again become theological. For a time, while many people believed that knowledge is power and while Goethe's Faust was altering St. John's gospel from "In the beginning was the Word" to "In the beginning was the Deed," it seemed that theological problems were no longer real. Men galloped ahead in the pursuit of knowledge and the

1. New York, 1965.
2. New York, 1967.

18

technical mastery which knowledge, so conceived, brought in its train. But suddenly, the technical power of the human race has become immense. The leading problem for biological scientists, geneticists, psychologists, engineers, chemists and others is not so much *"Can* we do X?" for it seems obvious that, given time and resources, we can do yet undreamed of things. The vexing problem has increasingly become: "Of course we can do X; but *should* we?" The weight of inquiry has shifted from technical problems to questions of values.

Thus, the value-free discourse of the last generation no longer suffices for human living. When men turn to imagine the cities of the future, they find themselves asking: "What do we think a man is like, this man for whom we are building the city? Which things are important to him? What, in the long term, are basic human imperatives, fundamental priorities? Which arrangements of a city most allow for the development of human potentialities?" We have moved from the area of discourse of John Dewey's social planning and pragmatic adjustment to the area of discourse of Aristotle's "architectonic,"[3] to questions of ends, to a metaphysics become (notes Marcuse) physical.[4] We have moved from what Péguy called *politique* to what he called *mystique*.[5] We have moved from technical considerations to considerations of values. We have moved from value-free discourse to discourse that is, in the largest sense, theology: a vision of man and his ultimate commitments.

Many, of course, will dislike the connotations of "theology;" they are, after all, atheists. But the word "ideology" has even less pleasing connotations: it implies, as Daniel Bell has argued, a rigidity of program and vision, combined with a passionate

3. *Nicomachean Ethics*, ch. 1.
4. Herbert Marcuse, *One Dimensional Man* (Boston, 1966), pp. 229–231.
5. Charles Péguy, *Basic Verities* (Chicago, 1965), p. 75.

19

dedication that borders on fanaticism.[6] It is bad enough to be called a theologian; it is worse to be called an ideologue. But a more important consideration is the following. The astute reader of theological discourse will soon discover that every sentence in such discourse, however obliquely, refers to human actions, or dispositions, or programs. Both Judaism and Christianity insist that men take their historical responsibilities seriously; both have theories of time that require the expectation of a future different from the present; and both insist that men must labor to prepare the way for that future. The "kingdom of God" is the prototype of utopia. Often this "kingdom" also has an otherworldly, apocalyptic concomitant; but it is in its own right a concrete, historical, thisworldly ideal. Theology is the study of ultimate visions of communal relationships and personal identity, insofar as these affect actual human experience.

It was the achievement of the generation immediately preceding ours to have replaced vision with pragmatism, ideals with compromise and adjustment, theology with technique. So effectively did that generation succeed that its methods swept the fields of government, churches, businesses and universities. The profound crisis of the recent world wars in which some hundred million persons died shook the optimism of visionaries. The cold war, with its threat of nuclear annihilation, inculcated a sense of ideological modesty, of adjustment, of restraint. The preëminence of the scientific and technological disciplines taught a whole generation of students the difference between descriptive and normative discourse. Rewards went to those who learned how to describe; discrimination between alternative norms was seldom undertaken and a radical criticism of implicitly accepted norms was disallowed. For value-free discourse leaves questions of values aside (usually by incorporating them implicitly). A pragmatic view of life

6. *The End of Ideology* (New York, 1965).

operates *within* a system of values; it seeks to bring about reconciliation and adjustment; it cannot call the whole system into question.[7] To indulge in ideology, or "metaphysics," or theology thus becomes suspect, subversive, and dangerous. Even Albert Camus, in *The Rebel*, found himself arguing for a reasonable moderation in the name of rebellion.[8]

Every historical movement bears fruit for the human community; pragmatism is no exception. If it is romantic and exciting to begin a new movement by bolting from the old while consigning it to hell, it is evidence of a larger freedom to be able to learn from the old without totally rejecting it; to replace it without relinquishing its benefits. The New Left sees in the Old Left much to admire. It also sees gaping inadequacies. The new generation is working to construct a philosophical outlook able to save the admirable qualities of the old while supplying for its deficiencies. A Christian theologian does well to commit his life to such an enterprise.

2.

The inadequacies of the old order have become apparent at four points: the questions of hope, evil, idolatry, and personal dignity.

(1) HOPE. The young think that those former radicals, professors, editors, and managers of our society who matured during the cold war do not hope enough. Because they do not hope, they surrender the quality of human life to an appalling irrationality. They accept life in a country almost half of whose wealth goes into armaments; they thus make the destruction of the world almost invitable.[9] Given the power

7. Marcuse, p. 172.
8. New York, 1956.
9. This irrationality is one of the basic themes of Marcuse's *One Dimensional Man*. See also Staughton Lynd in *The New Radicals*, Paul

and proliferation of nuclear weapons, it seems unbelievably complacent to rely upon a strategy of "muddling through." If we can destroy the entire world, the young believe, then the probability seems rather high that we will—unless there is made a far bolder and more energetic effort than anything so far proposed. Those now in power prepare the future; the lives of the young are directly at stake. The young hope to live. There is desperation in their hope.

Moreover, in the civil rights movement the young have discovered direct evidence of the power of hope. Against an immemorial racism, against a centuries-old pattern of acquiescence, the young dared to protest. They dreamed: "We shall overcome, some day." President Kennedy pleaded for the nation to "get moving again," and for the young to "ask what you can do for your country." The young did not, then, have to accept; they could question, dream, and act.

In this light, Albert Camus has become something of a danger to the New Left. "Camus was terribly important in helping us break through the immobilizing pessimism of the fifties," Steve Weissmann writes. "Now there is a fear that his philosophy can too easily become a pose." For Camus himself seemed unable "to move beyond nationalism" and to deal with the struggle of the Algerians for independence. Camus was not constructive enough; he did not imagine enough. It is time, Weissmann adds, "to get beyond *Weltschmerz*, beyond existentialist preoccupations."[10] It is time to build a new world. Yet the new hope is not optimism; it is hope. It is just enough hope to act on. It is a very guarded hope. It is a hope very close to despair. It is a hope that has discovered evil.

(2) EVIL. The young men who worked in Mississippi from 1960 to 1965 saw their friends beaten with whips by officers of

Jacobs and Saul Landau, eds. (New York, 1966), p. 314; hereafter cited as Jacobs and Landau in text and notes.

10. "New Left Man Meets the Dead God," *Motive*, XXVII (January 1967), 29; hereafter cited as Weissman in texts and notes.

the law. They noted in 1964 that white people were shocked by the murder of the white Reverend Reeb, although unmoved by the murder of a Negro youth in the same place only a week before. The young have labored for weeks in Newark to get a single traffic light installed.[11] They have felt the sizzling hatred of white citizens in Cicero, Illinois. From all such experiences, and many more, the young radicals have come to feel deep in the stomach that life in the United States is not reasonable, or open, or honest. They have come to experience in their own flesh the racism of American people, the widespread cult of a superior race, and thick insensitivity to the sufferings of colored peoples.

Moreover, the young who are called upon either to serve in the armed forces or go to jail have also watched their government become involved through half-truths, misrepresentations, and lies in an ugly and brutal intervention in a nationalist civil war in Vietnam. They have heard the United States speak of peace, while at every step taking the initiative in military destructiveness.[12] They have recognized clearly how high military spending ranks in the economic priorities of this nation, and how closely military industry directs technological investigation in the universities. The wealthiest civilization in history gives top priority to making war and making ready for war.

The young, in short, have a profound sense of their own complicity in evil, evil on a mass scale never known in history. Every dollar they spend—even on a fountain pen—might somewhere, under a different set of priorities, be saving the life of a child.[13] The system of priorities is irrational beyond

11. *Ibid.*, 23; see also Tom Hayden, "The New Radicalism, Round IV," *Partisan Review*, XXXIII (Winter 1966), 43–48.

12. Ronald Aronson, "The Movement and its Critics," *Studies on the Left*, VI (Winter 1966); hereafter cited as Aronson.

13. "One American spoke to a woman in Latin America who, since he had seen her, had lost another child. He asked who she blamed. Her answer was blunt: 'You! and all the others like you who can afford

23

belief. The United States keeps three million men under arms, and now spends vastly more in the destruction of Vietnam than was earlier spent, in those days when it might have helped, in peaceful and creative aids. Is justice, they ask, merely a pretty word?

(3) IDOLATRY. Perhaps the greatest shock to the New Left, the trauma in which its sense of identity was born, was the position taken by the leaders of the Old Left at the Democratic Convention in Atlantic City in 1964. There, instead of siding with the cause of the Mississippi Freedom Democratic Party, the leaders of the Old Left revealed that their prior commitment was to "consensus politics," to pragmatism, to the on-going enterprise of the Democratic Party.[14] Again, during the days of the Free Speech Movement at Berkeley, many of the young noted the prior commitment of liberal professors and administrators to the corporate status quo, a liberal status quo. They concluded that in such company one may tinker and adjust, but one may not question the premises. By and large, they felt, the performance of liberal professors regarding the Vietnam war manifested the same ultimate acquiescence.[15]

---

those shoes and that suit. I think just the money you paid for that pen could have saved one of my children'" (Weissman, 28, quoting John Gerassi, The Great Fear in Latin America [New York, 1965], pp. 98–99).

14. Howard Zinn, SNCC, The Abolitionists (Boston, 1965), pp. 250–262; hereafter cited as Zinn; Hal Draper, "In defense of the New Left," New Politics, IV, no. 3, 12–13; Norm Fruchter. "The New Radicalism, Round IV," 35–36 (see note 11); Staughton Lynd, "Coalition Politics or Non-Violent Revolution," Jacobs and Landau, pp. 312–313.

15. Weissmann, pp. 23–24; Joseph Paff, Bill Cavala, and Jerry Berman, "The Student Riots at Berkeley: Dissent in the Multiuniversity," The New Student Left: An Anthology, Mitchell Cohen and Dennis Hale, eds. (Boston, 1966), pp. 246, 250, 253; hereafter cited as Cohen and Hale; Marvin Garson, "Aftermath of the Berkeley Revolt," New Politics, V, no. 1, pp. 35–40. See discussion in Hal Draper's Berkeley: The New Student Revolt (New York, 1965); hereafter cited as Draper, Berkeley; Revolution at Berkeley, Michael V. Miller and Susan Gilmore, eds. (New York, 1965); The Berkeley Student Revolt: Facts and Interpretations, Seymour Martin Lipset and Sheldon S. Wolin, eds. (New York, 1965).

Thus there arose among the young a fresh analysis of the political situation in the United States. According to the Old Left, the number one danger is the resurgence of the Radical Right. Compromise, consensus and moderation are required to keep the Right quiescent. According to the New Left, the number one power in the United States is "corporate liberalism"[16]—an alliance of technical experts, well-paid professors and communications specialists, managers, staff politicians, professional social workers, and tycoons of the new technologically based industries. These people together accept the present system as a given. Many of them recognize its inadequacies and labor to change it from within. But they are well-paid by the system. They are its organizers, its leaders, its brains and nerves. They are its priests. The New Left could not accept this system. Of nothing do they speak so bitterly as "the establishment."[17] In the eyes of the New Left, the Radical Right is no danger at all, only a mirage by which the Old Left justifies its own caution, a devil summoned up to dramatize the continuing need for the sacramental system of corporate liberalism.[18]

Martin Luther said against the medieval system: "Here I stand. I can do no other." The young radicals say against the

16. Carl Oglesby, "Liberalism and the Corporate State," in Jacobs and Landau, pp. 257–266.

17. Tom Hayden, "A Letter to the New (Young) Left," in Cohen and Hale, pp. 3–9. Hayden makes the following comment in Jacobs and Landau (p. 4, 33): "The movement rejects the careers and life styles of the American Liberal, too, for to the movement it is the liberal way of life and frame of mind that represents the evil of America. . . . liberals have substituted rhetoric for content, obscured principles of justice by administrative bureaucracy, sacrificed human values for efficiency, and hypocritically justified a brutal attempt to establish American hegemony over the world with sterile anticommunism."

18. Weissman, pp. 24–25; Martin J. Sklar and James Weinstein, "Socialism and the New Left," *Studies on the Left*, VI, no. 2 (1966), 67; hereafter cited as Sklar and Weinstein. "The system is characterized mainly by its undemocratic manner of making decisions" (Aronson, p. 7).

American system: "Resist."[19] The issue at stake is whether the American system as presently established defeats the very goals it claims to stand for; whether, in short, the system has come to be worshipped in the place of the values which justify it. "Let God be God," Luther wrote, even at the price of division. "Let America be free and just," the radicals assert, even at the price of a renewed revolution.

(4) HUMAN DIGNITY. At the heart of every claim made by the radicals is a criterion of personal dignity: personal freedom. Corporate liberalism continues to employ the word "freedom," but the young do not discover much freedom in the inevitable choice they face between fighting in a war that they see as unjust and going to jail for five years during their twenties. Nor do the young see much "freedom" left for the Vietnamese by American involvement in Vietnamese affairs since 1945, and especially since the massive military destructiveness began in 1964. But neither do the young discover much freedom in the industrialization of the universities—grants and monies for the knowledge industry depend heavily upon research directed toward military purposes, in alignment with the present technological priorities of our society.[20]

The issue of human dignity, however, cuts more deeply still. The young do not think of life in a democracy as a matter of "social adjustment." They do not define themselves as "useful members of society" nor as individuals who wish to "make a contribution to society." For two fallacies would underlie such definitions. In the first place, a human being is not a means but an end; he is not even a means to the betterment of so-

19. David Ransom, "Stanford Observed: The Military-Industrial Park," *Resistance*, I, no. 1 (March 9, 1967). *Resistance* was the predecessor of *The Mid-Peninsula Observer* (Palo Alto, Calif.).

20. Bruce Payne, David Walls, and Jerry Berman, "Theodicy of 1984: The philosophy of Clark Kerr," Cohen and Hale, pp. 232–241; Mario Savio, "An End to History," *ibid.*, pp. 253–257; Barry Greenberg, "Misuses of the University," *Resistance*, I, no. 1 (March 9, 1967); Michael Novak, "God in the Colleges: The Dehumanization of the University," Cohen and Hale, pp. 258–270.

ciety; not even an instrument of consensus or harmony or smooth functioning. Society exists for men, not men for society. But, in the second place, the assumption that man is an atomic individual—one who, to be sure, "finds his place in" and "contributes functionally to" the social mechanism—is also incorrect. The primary reality of human consciousness is not the individual but the community; the individual person develops creatively only in the context of a community. Such a community, to be healthy, must respect the uniqueness of each person. Each person, to be healthy, must respect his brotherhood with all others. Community and person are interrelated and cannot be understood apart from one another.[21]

The underlying model for freedom employed by many thinkers of the Old Left appears to be that of atomic particles whose freedom consists in lack of restraint. Such atomic particles are impermeable by one another. They protect their freedom by manifesting tolerance for one another as they pass in their separate orbits or as they combine in cooperative functioning. For the New Left, such an underlying model is too mechanistic, too impersonal, too inhuman; in their eyes, it is ripe for manipulation. Someone, somewhere, rationalizes the system of particles and directs their flow, reducing tensions "creatively" by adroit adjustments. Freedom in such a system is only the appearance of freedom—such as academic people commonly seem to manifest.[22]

By contrast, the model of freedom employed by the New Left depends upon the sense of community and the sense of identity. These, in turn, are seen to arise from the conscious appropriation of one's own inner life—of one's own range of

21. See Michael Novak, "Moral Society and Immoral Man," *Church-State Relations in Ecumenical Perspective*, Elwyn A. Smith, ed. (Pittsburgh, 1966), pp. 92–113; and in *A Time to Build*, pp. 354–372.

22. See David Spitz, "On Pure Tolerance: A Critique of Criticism, a Polemic against Marcuse, Moore, and Woolff," *Dissent, XIII* (September–October 1966), pp. 510–543; see also the debate between Spitz and Michael Walzer, *ibid.* (November–December), pp. 725–739.

experience, understanding, judgment, and decision. In this sense, freedom is not given by the system through its lack of constraint nor by others through their tolerance. Freedom is seized from within; it is a matter of developing one's own inner life, of becoming awake to one's own experiences, one's own insights, one's own judgments, one's own decisions, and of exercising these with greater consciousness. From such a model derive the slogans of the radicals about moral feeling, *personal* knowledge, authenticity, participatory democracy and even—insofar as a rudimentary consciousness of community identity and community pride is a prerequisite of human dignity—black power.

It is not so much that the freedom spoken of by the New Left contradicts that spoken of by the Old; it is rather that the freedom of the Old Left is not sufficiently interior, not sufficiently personal, not sufficiently rooted in the inner growth and development of the human person. As a legal juridical criterion of action in the public forum the freedom of the Old Left is indispensable. The freedom spoken of by the New Left cannot be legislated; it can be exercised even in prison, even in a concentration camp, even—since it is the last citadel of human dignity to give way—under torture. In American society, millions who benefit from the freedom prized so highly by the Old Left do not exercise the freedom prized so highly by the New. Hence, the New Left argues, the hollowness of so much of American life; the vacant eyes watching television and drinking beer; the tired eyes of the men on the commuter train; the efficient eyes of the professor and the manager; the sincere eyes of the television politician. Americans, they argue, do not know who they are, only what they are useful for; they are bored and apathetic because they are manipulated; they are violent because they secretly resent the lies they are forced to live. Unable to live with themselves, Americans level the earth, build and destroy, attempt to master matter and space and human history. Americans play god.

That is the final reason why as a Christian theologian I support the New Left. Only God is God, and He is not a local God. ("Worship your local God!") America is not God's country nor are we godly and our enemies godless. The system under which America now lives is not divine; the "American way of life" is an idol. In this sense, to be a Christian one must be critical of America. For the old order of American life is inadequate. The American revolution is unfinished. More radically than others, the young have perceived our necessities. They will, if they keep up their courage, lead us to a new sense of personal identity, a new sense of community.

2. Identity and Intimacy

When Jack Newfield was a freshman at Hunter College in New York in 1956, he read a sign on a bulletin board: "Conform or Die."[1] All those who were in college in the 50's remember what it was like not to wish to get involved, to concentrate upon building one's own family and one's own career, to hope to take one's place within the system of American life. Moreover, in the classroom one was expected to be "objective." What *you* thought or felt hardly mattered: you were expected to show that you had acquired relevant information and could perform the necessary analytic operations as well as anybody else. You were expected to become a more or less sensitive computer. If you did, you would be rewarded with a high place in the system, and you could try to carve out a comfortable way of life for yourself and your family in a nice home in a nice suburb. You could, if you were lucky, live in the suburb of your choice. A college girl wrote during that period:

What we all lack, who are under 30, is some guiding passion, some moral vision if you will. We are unable to wind the loose threads of our experience into some larger pattern, and we know it. We write to please this authority or that professor while the universe skids about under our feet. We profess to disbelieve everything, partially because, at heart, we do not yet believe in ourselves. What we are facing is a process of re-education, of self-discovery —a painful process but without it no human being has understood the reason for his short walk across eternity—if our revolt seems

1. Jack Newfield, *A Prophetic Minority* (New York, 1967), p. 28; hereafter cited as Newfield.

mild, it is because we have not found anything to promote; deep in the dreams of ourselves in our relation to others, we realize with Yeats that there's more enterprise in walking naked.[2]

It was widely assumed that there was nothing especially wrong with America. But, then, in the 1960's, some young Americans began to try to win some small measure of justice for the Negro in our society. They soon discovered a great many things wrong with American society. They had hoped that with publicity, the people would be aroused and the federal government would come to the support of a cause that was just. Instead, they discovered how much hatred lay churning in the hearts of white people, how much fear in the Negro, and they learned the depths of the collusion between local law enforcement offices, the Federal Justice Department, and the United States Congress. They discovered that the pretty surface of America hid a very rotten core. These young people had no theory for such a discovery. "I curse this country every day of my life," said one of them, "because it made me hate it and I never wanted to."[3] The radical movement born in the 1960's was not continuous with any movement that had gone before. It rose suddenly, without forethought. It was born in moral shock. It arose out of a piercing and overwhelming feeling. It was a child of moral passion.

In February, 1960, four brave high school students in Greensboro, North Carolina, "sat in" at an all-white coffee counter. All they wanted was a piece of the American dream: Why could they buy pencils and paper at the next counter and not be able to have coffee like everybody else? Within the next few weeks, spontaneously and without any organization or any plan, sit-ins began all over the country, and rednecks carrying confederate flags where gentlemen had carried them

2. Dorothy Kosebud Doe, writing in *Assay*, University of Washington, quoted by Newfield, p. 27.
3. Newfield, p. 74.

once before applied lighted cigarettes to the necks of young girls at the counters. Hundreds of students were jailed, some were kept outside, several hundred of them were herded into a cage of chicken-coop wire in the cold winter air.[4] Then, that summer, Bob Moses went into Amite County, Mississippi, and began to register black voters. Fifty-five per cent of the population was black; only one black voter was registered. One hundred and seventeen percent of eligible white voters were registered. After Moses began to make slow, painful progress, the bravest of the blacks was shot to death, in front of more than thirty witnesses. Only one witness agreed to talk to the Justice Department; he could not obtain a promise of protection from the Justice Department, even though his life was threatened. He was soon gunned down with a shotgun. Later, Bob Moses was felled with a blow to the temple by a relative of the county sheriff and beaten into semi-unconsciousness, so that afterwards his friends tore his t-shirt from him, and wrung blood from it like water from a towel.[5] In 1960, none of these stories made the newspapers; America was not about to get involved.

There is no need to rehearse here the rest of the story of those next few years; it has already been done in many places.[6] The chief point is that the word "moral" came back into the vocabulary of the young. In the fifties, that word was very square and very suspect. In the sixties it acquired passion. One does not need to have a theory of social change. One only needs to open one's eyes and see.[7] The shock of what happens

4. Anthony Lewis and the *New York Times, Portrait of a Decade: The Second American Revolution* (New York, 1965), pp. 72–73; Newfield, pp. 35–39; Robert Penn Warren, *Who Speaks for the Negro?* (New York, 1966), pp. 358–361; hereafter cited as Warren.

5. Newfield, pp. 48–54.

6. See Zinn; Jacobs and Landau; Cohen and Hale; Newfield; Lewis, *Portrait of a Decade*; J. Simmons and Barry Winograd, *It's Happening: A Portrait of the Youth Scene Today* (Santa Barbara, 1966); hereafter cited as Simmons and Winograd.

7. Mario Savio, in a reply to Hal Draper, writes, "It is true that we

every day in American life was so repulsive that a new and powerful historical movement was born.

To be sure, even today, there are only a few radical young people, perhaps no more than 250,000 in this nation of so many millions.[8] But it does not take many to give an age a spirit, and it does not take many to supply leadership. "Give me one hundred young men who will live chastely and poorly," wrote Ignazio Silone, "and I will remake the face of Italy." This is not the place to sort out the many elements which make up this new movement nor to describe the process which brought these heterogeneous elements together.[9] It is more to the point to concentrate upon two themes of great importance to the movement, the themes of identity and community. We may take for granted, after the work of so many other writers, that these themes are of fundamental importance. Our aim will be to shed some light upon them in order to be of further use to the movement.

1.

The question of identity arises as soon as one steps out of the customary habits and routines of one's life, and can no longer believe what other people have told one that one is. For most young Americans in the fifties their identity was handed to

---

shall have need of all sorts of ideas and theories to set right these wrongs; but it is quite false to suppose we require a theory to see them. . . . I have a deep-seated suspicion of anyone who requires a theory to show that some practice is morally wrong. This suspicious aspect of my temperament may derive from early and painful training as a Roman Catholic. The church has a devious and elaborate system of ideas which goes to show *inter alia* that desiring pleasure for its own sake is evil! If something is *really* bad, it *should* be enough just to point to it" (*New Politics*, VI, no. 4, 14–15).

8. Newfield, p. 16.

9. "It contains within it, and often within individuals, elements of anarchism, socialism, pacifism, existentialism, transcendentalism, bohemianism, Populism, mysticism, and black nationalism" (Newfield, p. 16).

them. They were told that they belonged to the greatest and most powerful, most free, most advanced, and most superior culture in the history of the world. Moreover, they were told that at the cutting edge of that advance were the technicians and the business men, the professors and the progressive politicians—in short the white Christian middle and upper classes. The values of their own class had received no serious challenge. The affluence of their class seemed to confirm what they had been told. The proof of the goodness of the American system was its wealth and its productivity. Other countries by this same measure were underdeveloped and needed to be reformed.

But then hundreds of young Americans who went into Mississippi in 1964 and into other places in this country in later years discovered a pride, a courage, and a beauty in the lives of the poor that put the lives of their parents and their friends to shame. They met in America another culture; they met an underdeveloped country in the midst of our own country; and they came away shocked. The shock arose not only because the rest of America was hypocritical and did not really hold to the values it professed, justice for example. The shock was not only negative; it was also positive. The young found in the poor an alternative way of life, and there were things about the way of life that they admired as far more civilized than anything they had ever encountered in the world of machines and cocktail parties. When the young began to ask the question: "Who am I?" they found for the first time that they had a choice concerning how to decide the answer to that question. They would create their own identity; they could fashion their own destiny. They had not, then, merely been processed by some vast cosmic machine so as to show up on the production line at a given hour, and have their identity conferred upon them and their place in the system fixed. On the contrary, they had begun to read Albert Camus—Albert Camus became their number one hero—and they had learned the importance of deciding who one is. But until they went to Mississippi and into Harlem and Chicago's Uptown, they had not really had the opportunity to choose. They had not known in their own flesh and blood an alternative way of life. Now many of them in those early years came face to face with death. They saw dozens of their friends die.[10] Hence, the question arose: Granted that I must die, how shall I live?[11] Death seemed the inevitable end of the young, either in Cicero or Mississippi or Vietnam. As long as death or imprisonment lay up ahead, what did one have to fear?

Moreover, the increasing mobility of American life had already meant that the young were freer from their parents than any generation before in American history. Fewer families every year have lived all their lives in one house or in one part of town, or even in one town. In the resulting pluralism, almost all Americans now live next door to people who do not go to their church or go to no church at all; who have different explicit commitments than they. But all these people live in approximately the same way and so the usual ways of defining one's identity begin to seem useless. What difference does it make if one is a Catholic or a Methodist, a Baptist or an Episcopalian, a Lutheran or a Jew, a Christian or an atheist?

Thirdly, the generation that was reaching its twenties in the 1960's was the first in the history of the world to grow up with television sets in the living room. Vicariously, as a matter of daily life, they traveled to every continent in the world, were involved in international intrigue, murders, divorces, and every kind of adventure. Their emotions and their imaginations were deeply affected by such an education. In a very few years, they had lived a great deal. In effect, they came to school and said, "What else is new?" However, the universities that they attended were also increasingly demanding. And the

10. Warren, pp. 382–383.
11. John S. Dunne, *City of the Gods* (New York, 1965).

35

university had everything already mapped out for these young people; it planned to feed them smoothly into the system. Clark Kerr remarked in 1959: "The employers will love this generation. They aren't going to press many grievances. They are going to be easy to handle. There aren't going to be any riots."[12] Not many semesters later, Mario Savio was saying:

Many students here at the University, many people in society, are wandering aimlessly about. Strangers in their own lives, there is no place for them. They are people who have not learned to compromise, who for example have come to the University to learn to question, to grow, to learn. . . . And they find at one point or another that for them to become a part of society . . . they must suppress the most creative impulse that they have; this is a prior condition in being part of the system. The university is . . . well tooled, to turn out people with all the sharp edges worn off—the well-rounded person . . . and this means that the best among the people who enter must wander aimlessly . . . , doubting whether there is any point in what they are doing and looking toward a very bleak existence afterward in a game in which all of the rules have been made up—rules which one cannot really amend.[13]

These were the conditions under which the young people who reached the colleges in the sixties began to step back from the system and to ask: "Who am I?"

But what does it mean to seek your own identity? By what tests do you know that you have found yourself? What is it that you look for? This question is different from all others. There is no litmus test to tell you which is your *real* self. The reason why the question "Who am I?" is unlike the question "What is oxygen?" is that there is no possible way of getting outside oneself so as to turn oneself into a problem, into subject-matter for "objective" analysis. The crucial difference is that, at a certain point, you *decide* who you are; you *create* yourself. No one is God; no one creates himself out of noth-

12. Quoted by Newfield, p. 25.
13. Cohen and Hale, p. 257.

ing, and no one can decide to become just anything at all. But once one has (1) come to some sort of assessment of the range of one's own temperament, personality, and talents, and (2) come to some awareness of alternative ways of life, then one can choose to realize one among several possible identities. A man *is* not himself; he becomes himself, he steps out ahead and fashions an identity for himself. We make ourselves who we are. Either that or we merely drift and let our parents, our teachers, our society, our peers make us into what they want us to be. It is a terrible fate not to have chosen one's own identity; a terrible fate to have been made, like an object, by others.

How do I know who I am? There are two conditions for self knowledge; the first is inward and the second is to be met only in community. One must learn a secret inwardness, be willing to listen to the wind, care as much about one's own feelings as about the theories of others. A peril in growing up in America today is that a young man reads so many books, hears so many theories, that he loses his grip upon his own experience. His head gets so full of analyses of others and theories of others that he is separated from his own experience by a spongy, resilient net of abstraction. Modern education tends to cover all the ground without ever touching it. Jacobs and Landau write that the search for identity among the young

assumes a rejection of everything connected with their old identity and of the technological, bureaucratic values they see as dominant in American life. It is also possible that their difficulties . . . force these young people into seeking meaning in experiences. They think the ivory-towered men of ideas have cheated them, lied to them, and that action and spontaneous experience will show them the truth.

In order to become oneself it is indispensable to be able to hear the impulses, the terrors, the desires, the outrage, that proliferate and fructify in the depths of the self. One needs quiet,

37

the outdoors, distance, silence—the self, like a forest, grows with quietness. Too much activity deafens the inner ear. Many of the younger generation have walked before the dawn in the hills, felt the dew fall upon dusty Mississippi roads after dusk, spent long hot days and endless chilly nights in jail; they have had time to grow in quietness. They have learned to listen to selves that more pragmatic men push down and drown to death.

The second condition for becoming oneself, however, requires that one be able to listen to others. No man becomes himself in solitude. Men create one another; identity is a gift one man confers on another. Erik Erikson writes of this gift as "basic trust";[14] Reinhold Niebuhr calls it "common grace".[15] Two strangers bump into each other leaving a subway train; they step back and then forward again simultaneously; their eyes meet and they laugh. Later in the day, they happen to meet in a department store; they recognize one another and smile again. Even in so simple an event, human consciousness has broken through the impersonality of the subway train; two strangers have ceased to be inanimate objects to one another and have made each other in one small way into persons. Such a simple transaction illustrates what happens in more complex situations in which two human persons express appreciation for one another. When a man tells a woman "You're beautiful!" her beauty becomes a part of her consciousness. When one person trusts another, a unique and powerful human bond is created. When one person admires another simply for being what he or she is, then a new awareness is created, a new achievement of consciousness, in which both persons become aware of one another not as means to one another's needs, but as ends in themselves. Jack Newfield expresses this consciousness succinctly when he dedicates *The Prophetic Minority:* "To Linda, for being."

14. Erik Erikson, *Insight and Responsibility* (New York, 1965), pp. 69, 89, 179–180.

15. Reinhold Niebuhr, *Man's Nature and the Communities* (New York, 1965), p. 27.

One condition of becoming a person, then, is to be able to appreciate other persons. It is to be able to accept them as persons, and to be accepted by them (perhaps because one is able to accept oneself). It is to respond to others not for their *function* but for their *being*. It is to respond, not in order to win friends or to influence people, but in order to appreciate them as they are. It is to put others at the center of one's attention, to treat them as ends, and to marvel that they are what they are. It is to cease using people and to begin, perhaps for the first time, to notice them.

Wherever the functional point of view is discarded and the appreciative point of view assumed, moreover, fundamental ethical categories change. The word "good" begins to take on the connotations of "beautiful." An aesthetic rather than a prescriptive or productive standard of judgment arises. "Good" is not adjudged to arise from "doing one's duty" or from "producing results" of some kind. Rather, "good" arises from a manner of being and acting; it applies to the *éclat* or *élan* or radiance of personality. It signifies that the man so described has found himself, is realizing his possibilities in a harmonious way, is at peace with himself, is honest, authentic, and fully present in his response to others. The prescriptive ethic of Kant, the Protestant ethic of duty, the Puritan ethic of work, are overcome and the Greek word for "good," *Kalon*, "beautiful," reappears in ethical thinking. What ancient and medieval thinkers called "the transcendentals"—truth, beauty, good, being—become once again part of ethical consciousness. These four transcendentals are inseparable and serve to define one another. "He's beautiful, man!" means something like: "He is a man," that is, "He is *good* because he is *true* to his own *being*, and that is *beautiful* to see."[16] There is an Emersonian transcendentalist, even Joycean, quality to the

---

16. Simmons and Winograd, p. 13; *The Port Huron Statement*, First Official Statement of Students for a Democratic Society, 1962 (Chicago, 1966), pp. 6–7.

New Left.[17] But its roots (especially where contemplation is united with action) lie in Greek and medieval consciousness, before the rise of the modern work ethic.

2.

Inevitably, then, the quest for self-identity leads to the discovery of community. To some extent, a man needs at least *two* communities if he is to find himself. If he is a member of one community only, the inertia of human life seems to be such that his identity is handed to him too easily; social pressures tell him who he is. But expose a man to the possibilities of another community of life and instantly psychic energies are released, confusion arises, and the germs of creativity begin to multiply in the chaos. Segregation is a great human evil precisely because it is a narrow prison—a prison for both groups who are segregated one from another. Each segregated group settles for less than the full range of human possibilities. Each makes a clay god out of its own "way of life" and in the name of that idol cuts human aspirations down to size until each individual is mutilated enough to fit "in his place."

Genuine community, by contrast, recognizes that no one set of social pressures is sufficient to inspire the full range of human possibilities. Consequently, the test of the genuineness of community today is whether it generates in its midst members who criticize the community, go beyond it, and seek to keep it creative, self-reforming, and self-transcending. A community that loses genuineness ceases to grow. A community that ceases to grow holds its members in the grip of death; its laws, customs, and conventions no longer spring with the flexibility and vitality of understanding and open-hearted love but, dried out and withered by fear, bind human beings rigidly and narrowly in the posture of death.

17. Newfield, p. 90.

Genuine community has two functions. It is the source of reconciliation and basic trust, the fount of that endurance and courage and mutual appreciation which human beings confer upon one another. But, secondly, it is a source of restlessness, discontent, criticism and the fresh imagination of new horizons whereby individual persons take upon themselves the responsibility of standing over against the community in order to lead it to further growth. A community that lacks reconciliation destroys itself through fratricide. A community that lacks prophetic criticism destroys itself through immobility.

The relationship between identity and community is paradoxical. Genuine community exists for the sake of the development of as many free, self-defining persons as it can possibly generate. (To propagandize is easy; to educate for freedom is extremely difficult.) But, on the other hand, free and self-defining persons grow only through interaction in communities. Unless there is first a community, there is no language, no sets of values, no methods of analysis, no accumulation of information. In order to go beyond his community, a man must first learn from his community. A genuine community exists in order that its young may go beyond it; for if the young do not go beyond it, the culture of the community becomes immobile, and if in the past the young had not ever gone beyond what they had inherited the community would long since have withered and decayed.

The young talk a great deal about "community" and about "I-Thou" relations. Too often they have merely learned new words and too often they substitute dewy-eyed sentiment, a cloying feeling of mutual need, for "communication." One must be suspicious of anyone who finds community easy, and entertains "I-Thou" relationships merely by looking into another person's eyes. There are three marks of genuine community, and each of them is difficult to attain.

The first mark of genuine community is that each person in the relationship has a basic *independence;* each is able to function apart from the given community; each person in the relationship is an end and not a means. By this criterion, those who are wholly dependent upon the community for their identity and their functioning have not matured; they are incapable of genuine community.

Secondly, *communication* between members of the community—verbal, emotional, symbolic, functional—must be clear and open; people must be able to mean what they say and say what they mean. A community of love does not mean that persons always tell one another "I love you," for sometimes they will want to tell one another to go to hell. In a genuine community, one need not make a practice of telling others to go to hell, but one must be able to tell them so when one thinks one must. Nowadays there are perhaps too many specialists at frankness who quite honestly hate everybody else and conscientiously tell them so; but societies in which people hate one another while smiling pleasant compliments are even more intolerable. Open communication, dissent, sharp argument, passionate disagreement, and frequent words of mutual esteem, therefore, provide a second set of criteria for genuine community.

Thirdly, since no human beings are infinite, every community soon generates a differentiation of rules and offices. Even a couple in love spontaneously divide up the responsibilities arising from their love. The larger a community becomes, however, the more marked becomes the differentiation of functions and roles. No one can do everything; not everyone can do some things as well as others can. Since in the normal course of affairs, moreover, not every one in a community is equally mature or at an equal stage in the discovery of his own identity, there is bound to be some confusion of roles and responsibilities, a great deal of mismatching, and an enormous area of confusion. Life in even the simplest of communities is often very difficult. Men can scarcely live without each other, but scarcely, too, do they manage to live with each other. Communities characteristically begin with enthusiasm, develop in confusion and conflict, and either learn devices of reconciliation or disintegrate. The criterion for successful differentiation of function, therefore, is a very important one.

It seems to me that Professor John Rawls has stated this criterion in a useful way.[18] The third criterion we are looking for is *fairness*. According to this criterion all offices and functions in a genuine community must be equally open to every member of the community. A simple test is available to determine whether this equality of opportunity obtains. Let each man imagine that someone else might assign him to any one of the offices or functions of the community. If he would be willing to approve of the entire system on the condition that he could not be sure in advance which position would be assigned to him, then that community is no respecter of persons and is fair. Perhaps some such model as this implicitly informs the convictions of those who establish offices in their community which each person shares according to rotation—as when, for example, everyone at a summer conference takes turns washing dishes, leading a seminar, cleaning the lavatories and the rest. For a system to be deemed fair, however, it is not necessary that each person actually take a hand at every task in rotation. It may well be that some are better at some tasks than others; that some like what they are doing; that some are unsuited by temperament or talent or preparation for some tasks; and so forth. But the essential point is that the system as a system must not be arbitrarily and in advance closed to some persons in respect to some offices. The system of offices and functions is fair when it respects all persons equally, and when the differentiation according to offices and functions does not become a differentiation of opportunity for aspiring to those offices and functions.

This criterion of fairness eases one of the main difficulties

18. John Rawls, "Justice as Fairness," *Philosophical Review*, LXVII (1958), 164–194.

which the theory of participatory democracy has so far faced. Participatory democracy requires that every person's own voice be heard in matters which affect that person and the community as a whole.[19] The leaders of the New Left are aware that the theories and plans of leaders often subtly coerce, or at least deflect, the genuine voice of the people. Consequently, participatory democracy has often been impaled upon the following dilemma: either dishonesty or ineffectiveness. The leader in a given community may possibly come to the community with a more fully developed awareness of himself and of issues. Such awareness, in fact, is the distinguishing mark of a leader. But if he *manifests* this awareness he may too easily sway the community; whereas, if he *hides* it, he may be being dishonest with himself and with them.

It seems, then, that there are times in the life of a community when fairness requires that the less conscious, the more timid, the less theoretical, have an unstructured opportunity to articulate their own concerns and aspirations.[20] There are other times when fairness requires the men who exercise the office of leadership to *lead*—to invent, and to articulate, goals which accurately realize the heretofore inarticulate aspirations of the community. To perform a special role within the community is not *ipso facto* to be unfair to the community. Sometimes leaders must lead or else be irresponsible. Those leaders who do not share the lifelong experience of the community must be very careful lest they impose their own insights insensitively upon people who feel quite otherwise. But the American people, for example, correctly ask that their President some-

19. On participatory democracy, see: Jacobs and Landau, pp. 35–36, 123, 137, 143, 271, 272; *Port Huron Statement*, pp. 7–18, 47; Richard Flacks, "On Participatory Democracy," *Dissent*, XIII (November-December 1966), 701–708; see also the debate between Richard Flacks, Tom Khan, and Paul Goodman, *ibid.*, XIV (March-April 1967), 250–255; for illustrations of participatory democracy at work, see the case studies in Zinn, *passim*, and in Hayden, pp. 43–55.

20. Aronson, pp. 15–16.

times evince leadership and not merely follow in the wake of public opinion polls or the slow glacier of consensus.

3.

To summarize: The search for identity and the search for community are one and the same. A man discovers who he is both in solitude and in the company of others. A community is a brotherhood both of mutual reconciliation and of mutual criticism. A genuine community encourages its members to discover their own identity freely, even at the price of leading the pilgrimage out into a new darkness and into new, creative adventures. Without such freedom, inventiveness, and courage, the community petrifies. A community is genuine not by being soft enough to be established by easy sentiment, but by being hard enough to meet the severe tests of the following three criteria: (1) Its members are independent ends, not dependent means or cogs in a machine. (2) Its avenues of communication, dissent, honesty, and mutual esteem are clear. (3) Its differentiation of roles and offices is fair.

Stokely Carmichael was once asked: "Stokely, when the world is the way you want it to be, what will it be like?" He is reported to have thought only for a moment before replying: "Men will love one another." To love, men must first find themselves. To find themselves, they must find one another. Identity and community are both found by one same decision: a decision to live in a certain way, a decision to live open to both one's own self and to the self of each of one's brothers.

3. Wisdom in Action

"There is a time," Mario Savio has said, "when the operation of the machine becomes so odious, makes you so sick at heart, that you can't take part, you can't even tacitly take part. And you've got to put your bodies upon the gears and upon the wheels, upon the levers, upon all the apparatus, and you've got to make it stop. And you've got to indicate to the people who run it, to the people who own it, that unless you're free, the machine will be prevented from working at all."[1] The new generation of students is not afraid to act. They act out of immediate feelings. They are just beginning to grope for a program, and to articulate a theory of action. This third chapter hopes to contribute to a theory of action and to sketch some planks of a program.

1.

The New Left acts. Even without a theory, even without a program, there is still immediate experience and immediate feeling, and these have so far sufficed to launch a revolution. But even in terms of philosophical theory the young have prepared the way for a revolution. Commonly in the philosophical discourse of the last few generations it has been imagined that action springs from beliefs, convictions, theories. First one gets straight the content and the logic of one's beliefs.

1. Draper, *Berkeley*, p. 98.

Then one applies one's beliefs to action. Even pragmatism, insofar as it took scientific discourse as its model, tended (*despite its own intention, to be sure*) to separate ethical hypotheses from ethical action, and to separate both from ethical feelings. The view of human action adopted by the New Left is much more unitary. No dualism is allowed to separate the emotive from the cognitive. Action is not imagined as following from ideology; rather, the relation is the other way around. If ideology is to be acceptable, it must grow out of and remain in touch with action. First one feels and then one acts, and, only as needs arise does one theorize.[2]

Such a theory of human action, of course, has deficiencies, but it also has one important power. It is for real. It keeps one's feet on the ground. It keeps one in contact with one's own heart, instincts, and intuitions. In such a viewpoint, authenticity becomes the chief touchstone of moral excellence. Where is a man at? Is he present in what he says and does? Is his body on the line? Authenticity, while rare, is beautiful. The only disadvantage is that even a redneck, even a Nazi (as Albert Camus discovered in a letter from a German friend),[3] can be authentic. One can be an honest, passionate, intuitive masochist, or murderer, or thief. Authenticity as a moral criterion is primary and necessary; but it does not measure everything that secular sanctity requires.

The *source* of radical action is immediate feeling. The *goal*

2. "We have taken the initiative from the adult spokesmen and leadership, setting the pace and policy as our actions evolve their own dynamic. . . . The issues for which we have been fighting are so clear and so right, and the commitment we demand so slight, that we should expect much greater success. [But] there is no recognition that the various objects of protest are not *sui generis* but are symptomatic of institutional forces with which the movement must ultimately deal. . . . The challenge ahead is to appraise and evolve radical alternatives to the inadequate society of today" (Robert Haber, "From Protest to Radicalism: An Appraisal of the Student Movement, 1960," Cohen and Hale, pp. 41, 43, 47, 49).

3. Albert Camus, *Resistance, Rebellion and Death* (New York, 1960).

47

has been succinctly put by Carl Oglesby: "We want to create a world in which love is more possible."[4] There are, however, two main criticisms lodged against radical action, even by those within the movement; the movement has not yet been able to develop practical *programs* for the full-scale revolution it envisages; secondly, the movement talks as if it is working for *all men* but so far its appeal and its ability to communicate are limited to a very few. In a word, the movement is often accused of utopianism and sectarianism.[5] Why is it characterized by these two limitations? Is there some secret root which accounts for both limitations?

There seems to be. The movement has arisen from a large complex of conditions and causes; but one thing nearly every strand of the movement has protested against is the spirit of abstraction, the substitution of the part (usually the theoretical part) for the whole. In the name of experience and in the name of moral feeling the young have protested against "the system"—against ideologies, interpretations, theories, rules,

4. Quoted by Newfield, p. 90.
5. For examples of the debate within the New Left on this topic, see the following: Sklar and Weinstein, pp. 62–70; Dale Johnson, "Ideology of Campus Revolt," Jacobs and Landau, pp. 96–101; C. Wright Mills, "On the New Left," *ibid.*, pp. 101–114; Richard Flacks, "Some Problems, Issues, Proposals," *ibid.*, pp. 162–165; the debate between the editors of *Studies on the Left*, *ibid.*, pp. 267–279; Weissman, pp. 25–36; Aronson, pp. 3–19; Bruce Payne, "SNCC: An Overview Two Years Later," Cohen and Hale, pp. 86–103; Jonathan Eisen, "Only Connect: Reflections on the Revolution," *ibid.*, pp. 2–9; Jeanne Riha, "Birth Pangs of the New Politics," *New Politics*, VI, no. 2, 86–90.
For examples of the debate among the Old Leftists on this topic, see the following: Arnold Kaufman, "Where Shall Liberals Go?", *Dissent*, XIII (September–October 1966), 574–592; Irving Howe, "New Styles in Leftism," Jacobs and Landau, p. 289; Bayard Rustin, "From Protest to Politics: The Future of the Civil Rights Movement," *ibid.*, pp. 295–310; Tom Khan, "The Problem of the New Left," *Commentary*, XL, no. 1 (July 1966), 30–38; Bayard Rustin, "New Radicalism: Round III," *Partisan Review*, XXXII (Fall 1965), 530–536; Hal Draper, "In Defense of New Radicals," *New Politics*, IV, no. 3, 5–28; Michael Harrington, "Is There a New Radicalism?", *Partisan Review*, XXXII (Spring 1965), 194; *ibid.* (Summer 1965).

regulations, patterns, forms. They have protested in the name of a "something more" which has been overlooked: real people, real emotions, real institutions, including their own, of which "the system" takes no account. They have proof in their own lives that "the system," for all its footnotes and its securities, does not know everything and not even all, perhaps any, of the important things about becoming a human being in our age.[6] The reaction, then, is against abstractions and towards experience—a prototypically American reaction, a healthy and profound reaction.

The tragic flaw in such reactions, however, is that inevitably, experience, too, is only part of the whole. Besides abstractions of theory there are also abstractions of experience and abstractions of sentiment. Avoiding the spirit of abstraction on one front, the movement has not been able to avoid it upon others. Prophetic minorities in history commonly rectify a balance by cleaving to one clean line; and in doing so they cast a lovely light. But they are inclined to be inhuman, to move upon too narrow a base, and to falsify human possibilities by prematurely foreclosing them.

For this reason, one sometimes wishes that Dostoevsky had told the Legend of the Pure Protester to counterbalance the Legend of the Grand Inquisitor. While the Inquisitor knew that ordinary people prefer bread and games to moral excellence, the Pure Protester, in the name of ordinary people, often

6. "Look at you, blowing up whole countries for the sake of some crazy ideologies that you don't live up to anyway. Look at you mindfucking a whole generation of kids into getting a revolving charge account and buying your junk (who's a junkie?). Look at you, needing a couple of stiff drinks before you have the balls to talk with another human being. Look at you, making it with your neighbor's wife on the sly just to try and prove that you're really alive. Look at you, hooked on your cafeteria of pills and making up dirty names for anybody who isn't in your bag, and screwing up the land and the water and the air for profit, and calling this nowhere scene the great society! And you're gonna tell us us how to live? C'mon man, you've got to be kidding!" (Simmons and Winograd, p. 28).

prefers moral excellence to people. Purity, indeed, is a privileged breeding ground of intense hatred, contempt, bitterness, and despair. What begins in joy ends in disdain. What begins as brotherhood ends as moral segregation. The Grand Inquisitor fed the people mystery, magic, and authority; such inhibitors prevent people from living a full, independent, critical life of their own. The Pure Protester feeds his followers morality, symbolic protest, and authenticity; and these, too, narrow down the range of human life as it is lived. The gentle Christ, saddened by the Inquisitor's corruption of the liberty of the children of God, must also contemplate the demands laid upon those same children by the Pure Protester. Purity, in order not to be destructive, must be tempered by forgiveness, gentleness, a sense of one's own dishonesties, a recognition of other human ideals—even of bourgeois ideals, even of middle class ideals, even of coalitionist ideals.

Out there beyond the movement there is a huge void, barren of any pretense of thought or social vision. This void, moreover, is beckoning to the erstwhile radical to come and join it. The temptation is great, and in the back of our minds lurks the suspicion that some day we will, in spite of ourselves, be part of the hollow world. Consequently, the movement turns inward, in a frantic attempt to convert and rehabilitate its own before they are swallowed up. I have the suspicion that many of the student groups do more good for their own members than for those in the "outside world" they are trying to help.[7]

It is something striking to find members of the New Left arguing as bitterly as theologians (and evincing even *odium theologicum*), conducting themselves like self-righteous mem-

7. Dennis Hale, "The Problems of Ideology," *New Politics*, IV, no. 2, 93, hereafter cited as Hale. When the children of the affluent, given the opportunities of a college education, call policemen "pigs," they are telling these men of the lower middle class: "You're slobs and you always will be." There is class bitterness as well as moral pretension in that dehumanizing cry.

bers of a special sect, confident that their purity of doctrine and purity of life distinguish them from others. It is as difficult to be a secular saint as to be any other kind of saint, and only a few, apparently, achieve the goal. "The one tragedy," Leon Bloy once wrote, " is not to have been a saint." Most men share that tragedy.

2.

Let us suppose, then, that the radical movement desires to construct a new system of life in America, political, social, economic, educational; in a word, a more human system. Immediately, then, three questions arise. First, what goals are to be established? Secondly, from what human potentialities are these goals derived, and are these the most fruitful potentialities to call upon? Thirdly, what programs give promise of success in realizing these goals?

The first premise of the coming revolution might be established in the following way. The goal pursued by the new radicals is the establishment of a human community, in which individuals decide upon their own identity and the forms of their community life; in which offices and roles are filled in a fair way. The main part of such a definition of goals is that every human being is invited, upon encounter, to respect and to appreciate every other human being. If the community allows persons to live merely contiguously, like mechanical parts in the same social machine, it is less than a human community ought to be. Human beings are valuable; despite the use or disuse they make of their lives, they are beautiful.[8] If the radi-

8. "We regard men as infinitely precious and possessed of unfulfilled capacities for reason, freedom, and love. In affirming these principles we are aware of countering perhaps the dominant conceptions of man in the twentieth century: that he is a thing to be manipulated, and that he is inherently incapable of directing his own affairs. We oppose the

cal movement aims at building up a human community, its goal is a community that includes all kinds of people. Such a community requires a great deal of tolerance: the sun shines on the just and the unjust alike.

At this precise point, the moral purity of the new radicals is a two-edged sword. On the one hand, their power clearly comes from moral sources. Wherever organization, the authority principle, or status and symbol begin to take over from moral outrage, radical movements wither on the vine and the students drift elsewhere. Of this revolution more purely than of any other what Charley Péguy wrote is true: "The Revolution is moral or not at all." But, on the other hand,

---

depersonalization that reduces human beings to the status of things—if anything, the brutalities of the twentieth century teach that means and ends are intimately related, that vague appeals to "posterity" cannot justify the mutilations of the present. We oppose, too, the doctrine of human incompetence because it rests essentially on the modern fact that men have been 'competently' manipulated into incompetence—we see little reason why men cannot meet with increasing skill the complexities and responsibilities of their situation, if society is organized not for minority, but for majority, participation in decision-making.

"Men have unrealized potential for self-cultivation, self-direction, self-understanding and creativity. It is this potential that we regard as crucial and to which we appeal, not to the human potentiality for violence, unreason, and submission to authority. The goal of man and society should be human independence: a concern not with image of popularity but with finding a meaning in life that is personally authentic; a quality of mind not compulsively driven by a sense of powerlessness, nor one which unthinkingly adopts status values, nor one which represses all threats to its habits, but one which has full spontaneous fragmented parts of personal history, one which openly faces problems which are troubling and unresolved; one with an intuitive awareness of possibilities, an active sense of curiosity, an ability and willingness to learn.

"This kind of independence does not mean egotistic individualism—the object is not to have one's way so much as it is to have a way that is one's own. Nor do we deify man—we merely have faith in his potential.

"Human relationships should involve fraternity and honesty. Human interdependence is contemporary fact; human brotherhood must be willed, however, as a condition of future survival and as the most appropriate form of social relations. Personal links between man and man are needed, especially to go beyond the partial and fragmentary bonds of function that bind men only as worker to worker, employer to employee, teacher to student, American to Russian" (*Port Huron Statement*, pp. 6–7; see footnote 16 in ch. 2).

those who feel moral outrage are easily singled out among the many who do not. If five percent of the college student body of the United States is radical, the vast majority clearly is not. How, then, will the radicals relate themselves to the others? If their goal is a human community, these others will have to be included, too. How will we build a new society in America when vast numbers prefer things the way they are, or, at least, acquiesce in them? For every young person shocked to the depths by the sight of a police officer beating a white demonstrator, there are others who do not wish to become involved, and many others, too, who are profoundly shocked but who easily forget. There are not many who lie awake at night.

But a community of men, if it is to be for all men, must come to terms with the inertia of human beings, their thick indifference, their concern for the life and security of those nearest them, the ease with which they lie and deceive themselves, their deep laziness, their conceit. Moral outrage, then, may often become a luxury by which in the name of humanity one masks one's hatred of the people nearest at hand. The perception of Stokely Carmichael goes straight to the heart: White middle class students should not use the black community as a means of personal salvation, nor as an escape from the sickness of their own society.[9] Those who seek to bring about a human revolution must deal with the human material of revolution: human beings as they are.

Many of the New Left appeared in the earliest years at least to accept a Socratic moral theory. They seemed to feel that if the American people could only be awakened to *see* the evils in American society, they would rebel against them. As Dennis Hall remarked in *New Politics*, the New Left has a pronounced faith in the power "of public opinion to extort reform from the power structure, once injustices are demon-

9. Warren (interview with Stokely Carmichael), pp. 394-397; Bayard Rustin makes this point too, in *Partisan Review* XXXII (Fall 1965), p. 528.

strated, clearly, for all to see."[10] To a certain extent and in limited cases, this confidence has been justified. Television brought the hideousness of racism and the terrors of napalm into comfortable living rooms and student dormitories; the contradiction between visual image and deeply held values was so great that a façade collapsed and, for a moment, action followed horrified insight. But in the long run and in most cases, insight does not suffice. Many men are capable of seeing and not seeing, of seeing and forgetting, of seeing and not caring, of seeing and doing nothing at all, of simply refusing to see, of seeing something else. Morality is not, after all, written on the heart like words cut into stone; an inward look sometimes reveals nothing at all.

Besides having the ability to see, therefore, men need to awaken themselves to motivations for wishing to see, and to further motivations for being willing to act according to what they see. Insights are not deeds; intentions are not deeds; not everyone who is honest is also committed, and not all who are committed persevere. A movement which charges itself with leading a revolution in the quality of human life must deal with many kinds of men in many stages of their moral development.

Secondly, there is the question of human potentialities. The radical students are probably correct in identifying the sense of identity and the sense of community as primary human potentialities, in whose absence life is less than human. But one might also like to see them press harder for the need to liberate *that human drive to enlarge one's own horizon* without which a man cannot transcend his present state of development.

At this point our discussion becomes, unavoidably, more technical. I would like to enlarge upon the usefulness of the notion of horizon in expressing the moral ideals of the secular

10. Hale, pp. 93–94.

saint. By the metaphor of horizon, I mean to unite the conscious subject and the range of all he can experience, understand, evaluate, and do. A horizon is constituted by two poles, as it were, a point and the limits of vision from that point. As a metaphor for human consciousness, horizon is conceived dynamically; it is a system on the move. Moreover, the "subjective" pole and the "objective" pole are mutually constitutive. A change in the subject usually involves a change in his range; and a change in the "objective" pole (in the range of experience or understanding, for example) usually brings about a change in the subject. Thus a subject and his world do not stand opposite one another, in confrontation; they enter into each other. A man is already in-the-world, conditioned by it and shaping it if only by perceiving it in the way he does.

Four human operations, chiefly, contribute to the development of a man's horizon: experience, understanding, reflective judgment, and deciding. By *experience* I mean to cover all the data and stimuli of conscious life, both external like persons and sights and sounds, and internal like images, feelings, and dreams. Sometimes this experience is direct and immediate, and then I call it first awareness. Sometimes it is analytical or reflexive—we are aware of being aware—and then I call it second awareness. "Floor people" simply do what they enjoy, perform immediately, are first aware. "Ceiling people" watch themselves perform: "Here I am standing on the beach, listening to the pounding of the surf, feeling the wind blow through my hair."

By *understanding* I mean the act of insight by which we see the point of a joke, catch the meaning of a lecture, devise a strategy for dealing with a complex situation, see patterns and connections in another man's behavior. Often understanding is pre-verbal; it occurs in a flash and one may have to think awhile in order to find words for it, and sometimes there are no words. But, in its second moment, understanding becomes conceptualized, verbal, articulate, communicable. If too much emphasis is placed upon this second moment, understanding becomes like memorizing and playing logical games with words. If too much emphasis is placed on the first moment, understanding becomes romantic, loses its clarity and safeguards, and degenerates in the end into the exchange of mutually resonant grunts. The first moment of understanding (the personally acquired insight) is the living, vital one. The second moment (the word, the conceptualization) is the pragmatic, useful, scientific one. The two moments need each other for self-protection; but are not always at peace with one another.

The third crucial human operation is that of *reflective, critical judgment*. The question answered by the operation of understanding is, "What's the point? What does it mean? What should we do?" By contrast the question answered by the operation of judgment, though simply voiced, requires a much more complicated set of component operations. The question is, "Is that so?" and it demands evidence. Not every bright idea is a sound idea. It is the function of judgment to decide which of many possible understandings are in fact accurate. But to make such decisions one must have criteria. And criteria are, finally, personal. To make a judgment is to invoke a set of values—concerning what is to count as evidence, which values should be given which weight, and how to discriminate what is relevant from what is not.

There are, in turn, two common ways of making judgments. One way is merely to assert them, setting no special store by them, and remaining detached from them. The second is to commit oneself to them and to be aware that in making any judgment whatever one is choosing one's own criteria and values. In this sense, to make a judgment about any fact is to speak of oneself as well as of the fact. Men, in short, are inseparable from "reality." There is no such thing, in the end, as an impersonal, objective, neutral, non-committal point of view. One may merely *assert* a judgment, without committing oneself to it. But, even so, merely to assert is to forfeit responsibility while yet to incur it. For even to assert a judgment is to have chosen certain criteria of relevance and evidence from other possible criteria. To refuse to commit oneself is to be playing a game; it is to make oneself into a kind of recording machine in which various sets of possibilities are dispassionately mapped. Nowadays we have machines to perform such tasks; men are capable of further operations. No one should commit himself prematurely; but a life made up merely of assertions is itself a commitment, and not the most human one, not the most admirable one.

Finally, there is the operation of *deciding*. It is not enough simply to make a good judgment about a situation. There is the further question of "What are we going to do about it?" Marx was fond of saying that human intelligence is not called to reflect the world, but to change it. Speculative intelligence is but one moment of the same intelligence of which practical intelligence is another: "What are we going to *do*?" The new students are most correct at this point; they recognize quite clearly that a man has not revealed his profoundest values until he has put his body where his words are. Only in deciding does a man reveal how deep run his criteria for judging, those values that guide his understanding and his experiencing.[11] An inner dynamism unites each of the four operations.

11. "Most persons who lean to the left politically are moved by quite important feelings of solidarity for the impoverished, the oppressed, the debased, and all of suffering mankind; by a commitment to the general ideals of Western humanism, particularly, the freedoms of speech, thought, and association; by a distrust of selfish, competitive, individualism operating in the economic sphere (or any other); by a belief in cooperation and collective planning balanced against the necessity for individual consent; and so on. These, however enthralling, are not worthy of our allegiance as abstractions. It is their infusion into practical life which gives them true content and determines the extent to which we shall value them. The things we are for or against are quite simple at the level of abstraction; it is in the test of their practical meaning that we must make our judgment—not between good and evil, but the more difficult distinction between better or best, or the hardest choice of all, that of the necessary evil. Radicalism, it seems to me, does not exclude morality; it invites and is given spirit by the quality of a reflective commitment, the combining of our passion and our critical talents into a provisional position. To remove an idea from the plane of abstraction, it should be added, means to inject its meaning into our total life—to send telegrams of support to Southern students means to

Experience raises questions for understanding; understanding raises a further question for judgment; judgment raises the matter of decision. Only at the term of this dynamism is a man to be counted fully a man. In his decisions a man's identity stands revealed. Even his love is born of decision: for thou rather than for any other.

One's human development, then, may be articulated as the progressive expansion of one's own horizon. To live according to this expansion is to live according to "the reality principle." By constantly extending the range of one's experiences, understandings, values, decisions; by constantly stepping forward into the unknown; and by constantly taking risks, a man grows into and shapes both his own identity and his world. By contrast, to retreat from experience, understanding, judgment, decisions, is to refuse to grow; it is to constrict the circle of life and to diminish one's taste of reality. Experience alone is not enough, understanding is required; but not any understanding will do—one requires the discipline, the skills, the development required for accurate judgment; and judgment without action is a barren sepulchre.

A revolution aimed at releasing the potentialities expressed in these key operations will not, I think, do the human race any harm, but a certain number of shock-waves are bound to be sent through every organ of our society. In the light of the reality principle, do not most of us live quite stunted lives?

3.

Finally, there arises the question of political and social programs. American society has, like the Catholic church, a fan-

live one's solidarity with them, not to belie glorious phrases by private selfishness or tolerance of local discrimination. Radical program is simply the radical style as it attempts to change the practical life" (Tom Hayden, in Cohen and Hale, pp. 2–9).

tastic ability to assimilate its own critics and prophets. No sooner does a man speak harsh words than national television and national magazines cajole further statements from him, and soon he is lost amid detergents, mouth rinses, comedians, singers, and politicians. He becomes "a personality." He is "newsworthy." The young radicals need a strategy for defeating mass society and mass media.[12] And their goal, like religious goals, requires them in any case to proceed slowly from one man to another. If your goal is personal identity, responsibility, genuine community, there are no automatic means, no methods reducible to the routines of mass production. One must go on one's way, living one's own life. Here, too, the medium is the message and both the medium and the message are that each one's life is his own. Each must awaken and be converted at his own pace—no gimmicks will do the job.

On the other hand, the institutions in which men live affect the probabilities of actual occurrences of such awakening. The routines of mass production and the consumer economy on which they are based inhibit the unfolding of the reality principle at almost every point. The work that men do, the selling which replaces communication, and the daily tasks which establish their life habits, do not encourage men to find either their own identity or genuine community. They sell their talents; they produce objects; they accumulate goods. Having rather than being is the category through which they are led to evaluate the world. It is a radical question whether a capitalist system, even the modified socialist-capitalist system under which we now live, is capable of promoting the reality prin-

12. "Yes, America has an extraordinary capacity to absorb, vulgarize and corrupt everything, including its political and psychic opposition. The newscast denouncing the 'professional rebel,' Mario Savio, is sponsored by one auto company advertising its latest model, 'The Rebel,' or another company, featuring a pretty girl shouting, 'Join the Dodge Rebellion!'" (Paul Jacobs, "What's Happening to America?" *Partisan Review*, XXXIII (Winter 1966), 30.

ciple; it appears, rather, to stunt and to mutilate the human spirit. On the other hand, the socialist-capitalist economic system does tend to eliminate poverty, physical misery, illness, and other chronic sources of suffering, at least among certain privileged races and nations of people. If the socialist-capitalist system were not in fact racist, and did not tend to concentrate its most rapid developments among the already rich, its benefits might be more widely sung, or at least entered into the ledger against its human emptiness.

The union laborers in the United States, for example, do not starve; their children go to school. These accomplishments for the last fifty years must be accredited, even while one notes the racism, the narrow cold war politics, the passion for television and pro-football, in which the union man works out his life. One could almost cry out in anguish that the suffering and sacrifices of past generations have come to this: A grown man with a can of beer finds his chief fulfillment in a televised game watched by thirty million others, and believes our land free, brave, and just.

Yet a community that is a human community, it appears, must deal with the conditions of life so lucidly stated by the Grand Inquisitor. Many men do not want freedom but bread and entertainment. There is an urgent need for as many others to rebel as possible. The fact remains that many men do not, will not, rebel. The point of any realistic political program is not, then, to convert the world all at once to liberty and justice. It is to find the lever of power that will promote the liberation of a few more men every minute of every day; it is to create the kind of institutions in which, at least, there is room (for those who so wish) to breathe. One cannot hope that all men will join in this creation.[13] One seeks allies where one can. If

13. "The times are too threatening for us to respond as comforters of the oppressed. Keeping sentiments as our base, we must move ahead . . . [with] the changing of society . . . [and] that means politics . . . that means drawing on what remains of the adult labor, academic and

even only a hundred men are free and at work in genuine community, life on earth has salt and savor; lacking them, life is useless, stale, and flat.

One of the great practical needs of American life, therefore, is for a vocation to poverty, community, freedom, and service. The new radicals are in fear because they have no models they can follow for life.[14] For a few years of service, perhaps, but then, inevitably, will come the "sellout." How can a man be in the world but not of it? Not even thousands of years of theology have solved that question. A man must run the risks; there is no other way.

But there are, at least, two separate strategies. One strategy is to live a more or less separate life, sustained by communities of special intensity. This was the strategy of the early monks, some of whom, like the Benedictines, have been able to live according to their basic spirit for fifteen-hundred years. The hippie communities of San Francisco and elsewhere represent a kind of contemplative mystical order;[15] the activist communities represent a kind of practical down-to-earth reforming order.[16]

The second strategy is to work out a way of living in every

---

political communities, not just revolting in despair against them and the world they have designed for us. . . . Our gains will be modest. . . slow and exhaustingly complex, lasting at the very least our lifetimes" (Tom Hayden, in Cohen and Hale, p. 8).

14. "In their personal life style, their aesthetic sense, many in the Movement reject affluence and its associated symbols. . . . Their parents' desires to own, to accumulate, to achieve the status and prestige which go with material wealth, are meaningless goals to the children. . . . And to achieve a feeling of community, of life, they have been willing to sacrifice most middle-class comforts" (Jacobs and Landau, p. 5).

"The students do not have conscious access to the Judeo-Christian tradition in which their commitment is recognized as *the* calling of man. Their intellectual and spiritual suffering is often self-destructive because the tradition of celebrating their commitment has been rendered unavailable to them by the keepers of that tradition, i.e., by the church" (Myron B. Bloy, Jr., "Technological Culture: A Theological Response," *Motive*, XXVII [March-April 1967], 51).

15. Simmons and Winograd, pp. 13–18.

16. *Ibid.*, p. 19.

part of the actual world, in every profession, in every way of life. The equivalent to this strategy is a lay movement, organized and unorganized, by which committed individuals work within whatever corner of the system is given to them in order to wrest from it the closest approximation they can to the values they most deeply cherish. The radical students need friends in the business world, in law, in medicine, in government, in the military. A good man, as Flannery O'Connor reminded us, is hard to find; one must be grateful for help from every possible corner. It takes a lot of men in a lot of places to change the quality of life on this planet so much as by a featherweight. The effort required is enormous. It should not surprise us that, seeing how herculean the task and how absurd the system under which we live, many of the best minds of our generation have gone mad, and that many others have simply opted out.

We have no right to expect the world to be more than absurd. Even the sign of Jesus, the cross, is absurd, and the Jews still await the Messiah. Atheist and believer share the same night. Let as many as can work together in the night, an ecumenical movement of those who hope to diminish by a little the number of stunted lives.

4. Power, Disruption, and Revolution

The younger generation is struggling for new conceptions, not only of community and identity, but also of revolutionary power. They have discovered that under certain institutional frameworks, community is almost impossible. They have also discovered that the search for one's own identity requires an examination of the institutions which have shaped that identity. The relentless pursuit of self-knowledge leads ultimately to political consciousness. Self-knowledge is not a kind of inwardness; it is an awareness of the powers and dominations under which one lives. Consequently, in becoming aware of themselves young people have simultaneously become aware of the American way of life as "a system": a unique composition of economic power, class structure, political interest, and cultural myths.

1. The System

Culture is constituted by meaning.[1] When an anthropologist examines the ruins of an ancient civilization, he studies its artifacts, its documents, its cities, its burial mounds, and every available aspect of its life. He studies these remnants as if they were signs, and he reads them with all the empathy and acuity he can muster in order to regain the intentionality—

1. Thomas F. O'Dea, *Sociology of Religion* (Englewood Cliffs, New Jersey, 1966), ch. 1.

the understanding and emotional tone—which they once expressed. Even simple things are fraught with symbolic power.[2] A great many people in contemporary American society thrill at the sight of a huge jet plane climbing steeply into a grey sky; many others are thrilled by the first sight of the annual line of new automobiles. The removed, naked human heart has one significance for a primitive tribe, and another for a Catholic nun in the nineteenth century, and yet another in a society where the first four hearts were transplanted from human being to human being within the space of four weeks.

So long as one lives within a culture, of course, it is difficult to state the meaning of that culture. For the meaning is lived rather than thought. So long as one stands within the frame of a language, one cannot talk about that frame; as Wittgenstein pointed out, one can only mount the ladder and kick it away, can only *show* but cannot *say*. Yet just because the American way of life seems to be a system of meaning undergoing rapid transition, some of the factors that constituted the older set of meanings are beginning to come into focus. A new framework is coming into being, and the older one is receding toward a distance in which it may be spoken of. Still, to try to state the meaning which has constituted the American way of life for at least the last two or three generations is too formidable a task. It will seem easier and clearer if we try to speak about the meaning of American culture not in its most general structure, but rather in connection with a limited number of questions of economic power, class structure, and political interest.

Arthur M. Schlesinger, Jr., averred in *The Vital Center* that "modern science has given the ruling class power which renders mass revolutions obsolete."[3] But if revolutions are impossible, does that mean that we are trapped? Does that mean that there can be no new beginnings, no new radical upheavals,

2. Weller Embler, *Metaphor and Meaning* (Deland, Florida, 1966), pp. 27–44.
3. (Cambridge, Mass., 1962), p. 151.

no matter how badly things might go? For a long time, this country has progressed through and by means of a pragmatic consensus, a judgment that fundamentally we are on the right track and that at the center our direction is humanistic and progressive. There might be aberrations this way and that, mistakes here or there, as there would be expected to be in any dynamic society, but our center of gravity is such (we thought) that we serve as the leading edge of the western world. We were taught that the center of history lies in the west: in Palestine and Athens and Rome and Paris and London and now in New York. Nations were to be called developed or underdeveloped in accordance with the degree to which they resembled us.

From a theological point of view, Americans are Pelagians concerning the structure of our country. we tend to think that it is not and cannot be evil at the center. We habitually believe that American intentions are good ones, that America has never started a war, that America is always on the side of democracy and justice and liberty, that American officials are to be trusted until proven untrustworthy, and that Americans are unusually innocent, generous, and good in their relationships with other people. We believe that at home we are free, and that while there are blemishes upon our performance we are essentially committed to the rights of every individual, regardless of race, color, or religion. We believe that we are free and responsible citizens, in command of our personal destiny and of our common government. We believe that American instincts are so sound that evils have only to be pointed out in order that American public opinion will rise up against them in outrage.

Young people have been brought up sharing beliefs like these. They have been forced by events to discard them one by one, events which since the Korean war have exposed the inner life of America in an unprecedented way. Many in the younger generation have experienced America as overtly and clearly racist, even though Americans do not usually describe themselves as racist and even though Americans commonly make statements of principles and ideals which are not racist. Let us dwell on this issue a moment. To some extent, the cynicism of explicit racism, like that announced by Adolf Hitler, is much worse than a hypocritical, implicit racism; one could not accuse Hitler of violating his own most cherished and publicly stated ideals when he set the master race the task of eliminating the Jews. On the other hand, a latent, hypocritical form of racism is much more difficult to deal with because few people are aware of sharing it and few, even after rather serious introspection, even notice that they share it. In American culture, the meaning of the word "racist" is difficult to specify exactly. It seems clear that a great many people believe spontaneously that the white race is superior to other races, and that many people have spontaneous and profound emotional reactions when placed in close contact with people of other races. Standards are employed in measuring what happens to the white race and what happens to other races. Moreover, *individuals* need not commit specific racist acts; racism can occur in acts of the total white community against the black community. "When white terrorists bomb a black church and kill five black children, that is an act of individual racism . . . But when in that same city—Birmingham, Alabama—five hundred black babies die each year because of the lack of food, shelter, and medical facilities. . . . that is a function of institutional racism."[4] Many sophisticated Americans, of course, have come to recognize the degree of racism that infects American life,[5] but it is astonishing how many Americans there are, in the suburbs and in professional life and in the universities, who still do not recognize it.

For most Americans, the study of world history seems to focus mainly upon the history of the West and to terminate in

4. Stokley Carmichael and Charles V. Hamilton, *Black Power* (New York, 1967), p. 4.
5. Taught largely by Ralph Ellison, *The Invisible Man* (New York, 1965), James Baldwin, *The Fire Next Time* (New York, 1963); and Malcom X, *The Autobiography of Malcom X* (New York, 1966).

the history of America. It is basically a history of the white race. When this view of history coincides with the arrangement of political and economic power in the contemporary world, the suggestion cannot be repressed that such a view of history is highly ideological; that, whatever other value it may have, it also serves as a screen for certain economic and political policies. The war in Vietnam, coming as it does on the heels of short revolutions in Guatemala and the Dominican Republic, brought into focus for young men, who were being called upon to fight for them, the goals of American economic and political programs. As Richard H. Rovere has made plain in a recent, candid article in the *The New Yorker*,[6] an older generation of Americans grew up fighting in the defense of liberty against Adolf Hitler and then, somewhat less clearly, in the defense of the people of South Korea. It was possible in those days to view the spread of Nazism or of Communism as one might view the spreading of black ink and then red ink across a map of the world. It was the task of America to hold back that spreading ink. Yet the myths of Nazi expansion and Communist expansion were clearly enough grounded in actual events. As time has gone on, however, the power of the United States has grown to be so huge that the map of the world would have to show another color of ink: the slow advance of the United States, its military bases, its economic interests, and its political policies into the inner lives of other nations. It appears that the United States is no longer guided by the defense of liberty or by national self-determination. It seems, rather, that the policies of the United States are now aimed at maintaining stability. From liberty to stability: a shift in the goal and center of gravity. It appears that no revolution, anywhere on the face of the world, will be allowed to continue unless the United States approves of its continuation. America

6. "Reflections Half Out of Tree," (October 28, 1967), 60–100. Reprinted in *Waist Deep in the Big Muddy* (Boston, 1968).

appears to be the world's foremost counterrevolutionary power.[7]

The struggle against the Third Reich and the Communist powers altered the life of the people of the United States in one further important respect. During every war in the history of the United States up until Pearl Harbor, there was great resistance to the idea of military conscription; draft riots broke out when such conscription was imposed. Since 1941, however, Americans have accepted the imposition of the draft supinely. For more than a quarter of a century, Americans have become accustomed to the draft as a fact of life. Yet the shift in fundamental American policy, the shift from the defense of liberty to the defense of stability, has transformed the meaning of military conscription. Nowadays, the same rhetoric is used as in 1941: one is drafted in order "to defend liberty," "to serve one's country," and "to do one's duty." Government officials continue to defend the war in Vietnam as if it were a continuation of the war against Communism in Korea and Nazism in Europe. Yet it is a little difficult to believe that the National Liberation Front, which has neither a navy or an air force, and the North Vietnamese, with a navy of small junks and an air force of hardly three score fighter planes, pose a threat against San Francisco.[8]

Meanwhile, the war in Vietnam could not have become so large with so little political debate unless there had already been in existence a draft system to which Americans had been inured and now hardly notice. The escalation has been gradual and it has been accepted by degrees. At no point did there have to be a major policy change which might come to the immediate attention of the voters, as would have been the case had there been no selective service law already in existence.

7. Carl Oglesby and Richard Shaull, *Containment and Change* (New York, 1967), ch. 4.

8. Bernard Fall points out how much more difficult it is to promote hatred of Ho Chi Minh than of Hitler, Tojo, or Stalin in World War II. See his *Last Reflections on a War* (Garden City, New York, 1967), pp. 59–60.

Without even noticing it, American society has been organized along militaristic lines and the war in Vietnam, which so far as air power is concerned already exceeds the ferocity of the war against the Nazis,[9] could be drifted into without advertence.

In brief, "the system" of American life, as it has been perceived by young people, is racist, counterrevolutionary, and militarist. The "mainstream of American opinion" seems to accept the system as it is and to be rather complacent about its health and vitality. More exactly, American opinion seems in recent years to be showing signs of uneasiness—and symptoms of a bad conscience—but the policies espoused by government officials of nation, state, and city seem to be policies of repression. What many Americans see as the matter of great urgency is to silence "outside agitators," "pseudo-intellectuals," and other "trouble makers." Few seem willing to face matters as they are, and to begin the necessary changes.

Now in such a situation there seem to be two general lines of response. The traditional, liberal, pragmatic response appears to be that the direction of American life is essentially right, but that certain mistakes have occurred and certain temporary malfunctions have arisen in the machinery—bad leadership, inadequately informed public opinion, the failure of intellectuals, and the like. The advantage of this response is that it remains close enough to the mainstream of American discourse to seem "reasonable" and "responsible." The difficulty with this position is that it does share the same fundamental assumption about American life that the forces of racism, counterrevolution and militarism share: that the health of the nation is fundamentally sound.

The second line of response is, of course, a diagnosis that is much more radical. The technological revolution which has taken place since the Second World War has so altered the conditions of American life,[10] the radicals argue, that Ameri-

9. See Frank Harvey, *Air War—Vietnam* (New York, 1967).
10. See Marcuse's *One Dimensional Man*.

can society is no longer turned in a humanistic direction. Conditions favorable to liberty, justice, and truth are no longer the aim of American life. Personal integrity and the sense of genuine community have never been easy to achieve, but life in the United States is now so organized that they are, possibly, more difficult of achievement than ever here. Technology has given the state so much power in the formation of opinion and in the creation of those images and symbols which generate action that democracy in the United States no longer means what it once did.[11] The evils of racism run more deeply than we thought.[12] The mark of violence is more deeply set upon our forehead than we had recognized. The ambitions of imperialism are nearer to our heart than we had admitted. The inequities of our economic arrangement divide us more thoroughly into classes than our rhetoric allows us to believe.[13]

The conclusion of this line of reasoning is that evolution is not sufficient; there must be a fundamental change in direction. Those who propound this more radical analysis wish to differentiate it from the liberal, pragmatic analysis which is evolutionary. The only word which remains at hand, once evolution is rejected, is "revolution." But what content can be given to that word in American life two centuries after the original revolution of 1776?

2. The Revolution

Once a pragmatic and realistic tradition has taken hold—a tradition in which compromise and adjustment are the ordi-

11. See Robert P. Wolff, Barrington Moore, Jr., and Herbert Marcuse, *A Critique of Pure Tolerance* (Boston, 1965).

12. See Tom Hayden, *Rebellion in Newark* (New York, 1967).

13. See Robert Heilbroner, "Who's Running the Show?", *New York Review of Books*, IX, no. 12 (January 1968), 18–21. (Review of G. William Donhoff, *Who Rules America* and Arnold M. Rose, *The Power Structure.*)

nary procedural methods—the word "revolution" sounds extraordinarily romantic. Whether one thinks of the Bastille, the barricades of 1848, or the galloping Cossacks of 1917, the imagery associated with "revolution" clashes much too harshly with our experience of American life. Yet once young men have been awakened from their pragmatic slumbers, no other word will quite do, even though the armed forces of the United States, together with the many police forces of the country, make any sort of armed uprising seem futile.

There is a second meaning of revolution which has also come to seem empty: the meaning of revolution which is the political equivalent of a moral conversion. We might call this meaning the Socratic meaning: it is the tendency to believe that knowledge is virtue, that awareness of evils is identical with the will to uproot evils. At the beginning of the civil rights movement, a great many young idealists seemed to believe that to alter the age-old injustices of American life it would suffice to expose these injustices to the plain view of the American people. The newspapers and television would show the country what was actually happening. And, outraged, the American citizen would set about making matters right. To change the direction of America, all one had to do was change the awareness of Americans. Such naïveté was short lived.

On the one hand, a revolution by the force of arms and in the romantic, European tradition does not seem probable, realistic, or desirable. On the other hand, a revolution through greater public awareness has proved to be illusory. What then is left? If it were not for the war in Vietnam, it might well be that the need for revolutionary thinking would appear to be much less pressing. Yet the war places a burden of death and decision immediately upon the shoulders of the young. They are faced with military service in support of a cause they find to be both illegal and immoral. Moreover, their analysis of American society teaches them that the war is not merely a mistake, not an accident which a different sort of leadership

71

might have avoided, but a strikingly clear exemplification of the fundamental direction of the mainstream of American life. Since the war faces them with a kind of involuntary servitude, and possibly with death or the need to kill, they experience the sort of desperation from which alone, it seems, a revolutionary frame of mind derives.[14] Since some of them are going to go to prison, or to die anyway, it does not seem to them unrealistic to stake everything upon the possibility of bringing about a change of direction in American life. But what sort of change shall this be? What kind of strategy should be adopted in order to effect it? In what new direction ought America to be turned?

The first requirement of revolutionary action is to bring more and more others to "revolutionary consciousness." Those who have come to see how profoundly their lives have been shaped by "the system," and how deeply it has insinuated itself into their sense of their own identity, need first to bring others to this same state of consciousness. Most young people did not come to "revolutionary consciousness" by thinking about it; it is not something that they were taught by their professors. They learned it by acting against the system. At one point or another, whether in the pursuit of civil rights or in an effort to bring about certain reforms in the university, they came face to face with attitudes, myths, and unyielding policies which they could not share. They discovered that beneath the idealism, the principles, the rhetoric, and the complacent good conscience of American society—even the most liberal and reasonable elements of American society—there was a hard core of resolute and unquestionable inhumanity. Moreover, when challenged, this inhumanity was defended not with reason but with the application of counterforce. At the end of every argument there was the barrel of a gun: a policeman's club, a censure, a suspension, a dismissal, a jail

14. Regis Debray stresses the power of desperation in *Revolution in the Revolution* (New York, 1967).

sentence, the spraying of mace, the employment of tear gas, the charging of a phalanx of policemen. To less innocent young people, the fact that society is based upon force would not have come as a surprise. The experience of being at the wrong end of the barrel of a gun is, however, the most formidable "radicalizing" tactic that middle-class students in America have yet discovered. Consequently those who are already radical constantly try to drive the flexible, resilient, pragmatic American system into crises of naked confrontation, and they try to bring as many other students into the experience of this confrontation as they can. Those who pass through it are never the same afterwards.

Overt violence is so far unacceptable; awareness gained through ordinary educational means is ineffectual. The tactics of disruption have proven extraordinarily fruitful. Moreover, without young men the American army simply cannot function, and so the issue of the selective service has been seized upon as the point in the system where (it is thought) the young have real power, and where the application of power can have a maximum effect. Resistance to the draft has become the most tangible and realistic way of bringing some young men to a sense of their own identity, a willingness to stand by their own integrity, and a sense of comradeship and community with others who are in danger. Resistance to the draft can at one and the same time be nonviolent and disruptive; it brings about a highly emotional and inwardly seering confrontation without resort to violence. Moreover, it draws upon and it also nourishes the widespread resistance to war and what the war stands for in American life. On the other hand, President Johnson ordered one hundred FBI agents to break the back of the resistance movement; district attorneys are arraigning more and more anti-draft demonstrators. The number of resisters seems to be far too few.

Still, resistance to the selective service system is only one front on which the battle must be fought to change the direction of American life. The university campus promises free speech to any who come to argue their views according to the conventions of reasonable discourse. At the present moment in history, however, government officials employ the rostrum on university campuses, not for purposes of reasonable argument and discourse, but to announce the official views of the government. Representatives of the Central Intelligence Agency and of the producers of war materials come to the campus, not to argue for the merits of their respective activities, but to recruit candidates for their ranks. Radical students wish to confront the government officials and the recruiters and make them argue for their positions, face to face, in the traditions of the university. But government officials commonly insist upon rigging the rules of the debate so that they will never be embarrassed, and the recruiters do not come to argue but to recruit. In their desperation, the radicals believe that the conventions of reasonable discourse have been abandoned, and that they must face the employment of power with power. They try to bring about a confrontation, hoping thereby to involve other students in their vivid contest against the industrial state.

Nevertheless, the tactics of disruption are contrary to the traditions of this country, and the prejudice of Americans weighs heavily in favor of officials so long as they act with decorum; thus the radical students seem to reap as much divisiveness and illwill as further radicalization. Moreover, if it is true that the conventions of reasonable discourse have actually broken down in our society, then the logic of disruption is actually the logic of armed revolution. If you really want to halt a local induction center, then you must employ means commensurate with your aim. Against armed ranks of policemen, a grenade is more serious and effective than calling names.

Still, young people who hope to make a revolution in the name of humanity come face-to-face with the major ethical dilemma of all such revolutionaries in our century: is it right to kill a human being in the name of his and one's own humanity?[15] If you turn to armed violence, are you any better than those whose policies have outraged your own moral sensitivities? If one accepts the fact that political life is a balance of powers, gun barrel against gun barrel, then the moral claims of humanism seem to be diminished. For if man is, in fact, incapable of community and reasonable discourse as a means of reconciling differences, then all the revolutions in the world are not going to alter that fact. There is no longer any room for moral outrage of an innocent and direct sort. Faced with a balance of forces, one may either try to accumulate more force so as to bring opposing powers into equilibrium, or one may try to preserve an always precarious stability.

The conflict in the consciousness of young radicals is extraordinarily poignant. On the one hand, they find the present direction of American life intolerable. On the other hand, they also find the logic of revolutionary consciousness, in so far as it ultimately leads to armed violence, intolerable. If they try to reconcile themselves to the second point of the dilemma, namely, to the fact that every social arrangement involves them in violence and even in murder,[16] then they may commit themselves to armed violence; but in the same stroke, they lose the ground on which their own humanistic aspirations were rooted. If they try to reconcile themselves to the first horn of the dilemma, namely, to the fact that the present system is corrupt as all systems inevitably are, they have to absorb a guilt and a responsibility that they are ill prepared to absorb. For they have not been taught that American society is guilty and corrupt, but that it is just and free and noble.

Moreover, the young have moved rapidly from ethical and

15. See for example, Irving Howe, *Politics and the Novel* (New York, 1967), ch. 8.

16. Paul Hanly Furfey, *The Respectable Murderers* (New York, 1966).

abstract issues to practical, political issues. Here their frustration is even more intense. One young man, having read an earlier version of this paper, recently typed me a note which read, in part: "Many are no longer asking whether they can kill as an ethical question, but as a political question, and *this* is the most frustrating problem. Who can you kill in this country so that it makes any difference? So what if you kill Johnson and Rusk and Rostow and Humphrey and all the Chiefs of Staff? There are thousands more who are scrounging for their positions and will carry out the same, if not more repressive, policies. And so what if you kill two hundred Oakland policemen with a grenade? The military in this country is strong enough to kill everyone who doesn't wear a uniform. So where can we turn? There are many dropping out every day."

The radical movement, therefore, has reached a point of hesitation. The most sensitive radical students ask themselves, alone and in the night, and occasionally in conversation: "Am I capable of killing another man? Can I live with myself if I shed the blood of others?" In an earlier generation of humanists, Sartre and Camus and others wrestled with this question; but they did so when the enemy was a clear and present aggressor, cynical and thorough in his methods of repression and his commitment to violence. When the Nazi tide had receded, Camus at first felt the same instincts of retribution and vengeance against those Frenchmen who had collaborated with the Nazis; in a short time, he changed his mind.[17] And he began to argue in *The Rebel* that in the choice between an ideology and a human life one must always choose in favor of the human life; this was the lesson to be learned from the ideological wars of our country. But the lesson of *The Rebel* could only be learned after the first lesson of resistance through armed violence had also been learned and had been proven

17. See Emmett Parker, *Albert Camus: The Artist in the Arena* (Madison, Wisconsin, 1966), p. 95; and Albert Camus, *The Rebel* (New York, 1956).

successful by victory. To which Camus should the young American turn, the Camus of 1942 or the Camus of 1945? The issue is not abstract. Next month, this summer, next year, violence may again erupt in American cities. A young man may well think: "If I am going to die in Vietnam anyway, why not die on the side of the revolution in America?" Such a stray thought is not at first taken seriously; it is too romantic, too un-American. But it returns like a haunting nightmare.

3. Identifying the Enemy

What is a Christian theologian to say about the dream of violence? Christianity began in an act of violence, and its first act was to show that violence, no matter what its sources, can be redemptive. If the Word who reveals to us God's nature and our own is to be understood, the Christian must confront the naked power of violence in every human situation. Nietzsche's accusations against Christianity must not be allowed to stand: the Word does not reveal that human life is pastoral, peaceful, nice, genteel, or reasonable but that it is violent. Blood runs down the wood of the cross. On the other hand, woe to them by whom the blood is made to run! The revolutions of 1776, of 1789, of 1848, of 1917 have been affairs of blood. Good has been brought forth from them, although at immense cost. It is impossible to deny the fact that—in Hegel's words—history is a butcher's bench. The first word must be that revolution, even a bloody revolution, is not *a priori* to be judged immoral.[18] All the more is this true because *every* social order rests upon a base of violence,[19] covert or overt, orderly or anarchistic. Politics is not a science of reason but of power.

To judge the morality of violence, one must think con-

18. Raghavan Iyer, "The Ethics of Revolution" in *The Center Magazine*, I, no. 2 (January 1968), 85–88.

19. Reinhold Niebuhr, *Moral Man and Immoral Society* (New York, 1960). This book, first published in 1932, is relevant again.

cretely. "Revolution" is too large an abstraction. By whom? When? Where? To what end? By what means? To take up the banner of violence is to invoke violence in return. The revolutionary must think clearly, under pain of romantic gesture-making.

There are many different kinds of revolutionary situations, many different kinds of revolutionary method, many different kinds of revolutionary person.[20] What, roughly (it is impossible to be "precise" in any normal sense), is the situation in the United States in the present decade? The feature of American life most disheartening to the young, if I read them correctly, is the tyranny of an immoral majority—a majority that would prefer to wage war upon a mythical enemy embodied in other races in other nations, rather than to face its own rotten core and incipient civil war at home. The state of American cities, the relationships between Americans of differing races, the general pursuit of mere expertise and the wealth that flows from it—these grave moral illnesses are not met by a majority with the will to alter its way of life. The majority remains unmoved. In this light, proof is given that democratic processes in fact are subject to the poisons of irrationality, corruption, and evil, as other systems of government are. It is not true that majority rule necessarily leads to freedom. It is conceivable—it seems to be the case in America today—that a democratic majority would systematically prefer a high standard of living to justice, freedom, and truth: bread and circuses to adult responsibility.

When young Americans attack "the system," therefore, they are not necessarily attacking every institution, procedure, or achievement carried along by the American tradition. A great deal would be gained if this point could be made plain. The revolution of which the young speak, it is true, sometimes carries a nihilistic ring: burn down everything, destroy,

20. Flexibility in analysis is Regis Debray's fundamental point in *Revolution in the Revolution.*

halt, stop. The more accurate and commendable impulse, however, contains both a positive and a negative note. On the one hand, the inadequacy and hypocrisy of the present democratic machinery—chiefly due to the preference of Americans for a high standard of living over every other consideration—deserve to be sharply denounced. On the other hand, the tradition of free inquiry, integrity of conscience, compassion for the suffering, community with all men, and rule of the people by the people for the people must be *extended*. If there is need for a revolution in America (even perhaps a bloody revolution), it is in continuity with the revolution of 1776, not in denial of it. The morally genuine impulse of revolution is a forward movement: it is to be a revolution in the name of human values now and in the future.

The great hope of the liberals is that such progress can be achieved without bloodshed. But such hopes rest upon the assumption that a majority of the American people either now have or can be led to have the wisdom and the will to make the inherited democratic processes work. The new left has been led to doubt that assumption. The new left has lost faith in the American majority. This loss of faith is very recent; its taste is bitter and painful. When the present mood passes, however, it will not be enough merely to hate. Alternatives must be imagined, programs created, and actions launched. It is far easier to destroy than to create. I do not think the new left desires to be merely self-indulgent.

The enemy in America, then, is the tyrranical and indifferent majority: the good people, the churchgoers, the typical Americans, the ones who have been taught that to be an American is by that very fact to be moral, just, free, generous, and trustworthy. So long as such a majority controls the destiny of America, it appears, the nation will remain militarist, racist, and counterrevolutionary; the wealth of the United States will increase; conscience will be suffocated; the wretched of the earth will suffer yet more. The revolutionary problem is how to fight the moral sickness of the democratic majority: a revolutionary problem unique (so it seems) in history. It would be a grave mistake to destroy the machinery of democratic *process*, if it is true that the enemy is the democratic majority. The system of representative government, so far as it goes, is healthy; *it does not go far enough* and that is what makes it function as if it were sick. Moreover, the mechanisms by which our democratic processes were thought to be self-reforming have proven, instead, to be lamentably inadequate. Pragmatic adjustment of the available machinery is no longer sufficient. The democratic process needs a further extension, and the mechanisms of reform need extension: which is to say, much more rapid means of change are required.

Yet how can one rearrange the power bases of American democracy, both economically and politically, so that changes can come rapidly and effectively? It seems futile to believe that a majority of Americans will be persuaded by reasonable argument or by the manipulation of public opinion to consent to such a rearrangement. It is at this point that tactics of disruption become feasible. The American majority must be shown how desperately inadequate our society is; and they themselves must be placed, for a change, in the line of fire. To be sure, persons who are threatened may respond with repressive violence; further, it is wishful thinking to imagine that the later contemplation of their violence will move them to regrets. Yet if the democratic majority represses disruption with force, then at least the heretofore covert violence of the respectable will become overt. There is an undeniable satisfaction in making hypocrisy yield to honesty. Yet such satisfaction is not political power. Disruptive tactics seem to have as their premiss either (a) that the democratic majority can yet be shocked into mending its ways; or (b) that disruptive confrontation is an indispensable first step in a long-term revolutionary process, insofar as it serves to increase the number of those who are aware of the role of naked force in a society which likes to pretend that it is reasonable and free.

The notion that a revolution is a long-range project, meanwhile, relieves some of the emotional stress which members of the new left commonly feel. It is easier to keep cool if not every day is regarded as the last. Like early Christianity, the new left sometimes suffers from an eschatology whose fuse is unconscionably short. Patience, nonetheless, is the first virtue of the revolutionary. His courage is proved more thoroughly in steady endurance than in flashes of instantaneous action. Moreover, though the question of the employment of arms and open violence must remain open, it does not follow that violence is the only or even the ordinary method of the revolutionary. The opposite, in fact, seems to be the case. Most of the actions of the revolutionary are aimed at schooling himself in the aims of the revolution, so that others will find him trustworthy and so that others will learn by the way he lives the meaning of the revolution. Without the establishment of a community of revolutionary consciousness and trust, living by the ideal of the society of the future, no revolution worthy of the name can succeed. In the beginning, the forces of revolution are weak and the forces of tyranny (even the tyranny of a democratic majority) appear to be immovable.

In the United States at the present time, the moment has clearly not arrived for armed revolution. Riots in the cities may well be a foretaste of what is ahead, and those who serve now in the Army may one day be grateful to have learned military skills. At the present moment, more than anything else, the new left requires fresh economic, political, and social imagination, so as to imagine the manifold ways in which the genuine achievements of American society can be extended. To displace the democratic majority whether by changing the minds of a great many people or by so altering political and economic relationships that the present majority is fragmented, almost certainly will require strategy and tactics not presently part of the normal processes of change in our society. If we proceed with coolness and skill, the revolution will not be a step backward; if we are blessed, it may be a long step ahead.

5. Students and Demonstrations

One would have thought, a few years ago, that the age of ideology was at an end. But now young people have discovered that pragmatism, too, has the characteristics and effects of an ideology. They have observed, in particular, low resistance to a new, toughened strain of tyranny. Technological progress demands stability and unity over periods of time long enough to bring plans and projections to fulfillment; it thus depends upon control over natural resources, industrial facilities, future human desires, and world conditions.[1] Any government dedicated to the uses of advanced technology finds it in the national interest to produce and to enforce stability ("controlled dynamic growth") on a worldwide scale.

Thus university students have been among the first to discern and to condemn the dangers of the philosophy heretofore dominant in the intellectual life of this country. Many among the brightest and most emotionally mature students, as studies like that of Joseph Katz[2] have shown, are won over by the experiences, emotions and arguments that have given birth to the New Left. These are the students who rebel most strongly against liberal professors, liberal journals, and the general civilty and temperateness of liberalism. Moreover, so sharp is this rebellion that communication between Old Left and New Left is scarcely possible. Fundamental presuppositions

1. See John Kenneth Galbraith, *The New Industrial State* (Boston, 1968).
2. *Growth and Constraint in College Students* (Stanford, California, 1967).

have been changed. Basic value judgments are made differently. If we had an accurate map of what is at stake, perhaps it would become possible to disagree with clarity and precision, instead of with rudeness, contempt, and theological odium.

The argument of the students, naturally enough, is grounded in what they see and hear daily at the universities. The war in Vietnam has taught them that their professors share the basic values and interests of the American government and of the leaders of the new technological industries, whatever the highly publicized public differences between academy and town on questions of procedure. Thus the recent statement by fourteen "moderates"[3]—some of them giants in academic life—justifying present United States policy in Asia reaches the students as no surprise. They have long known what William Pfaff recently wrote in *Commonweal:* that the war in Vietnam is essentially a pragmatist's war, essentially a liberal war.[4] Protest against the war was slow in coming, precisely because it fitted the American intellectual temper so well.[5]

What, then, is the American intellectual temper as students perceive it? First, let us again be clear that we are talking about a minority of students, although probably the most significant minority in terms of perception and talent; and a growing minority. Secondly, we need a context in which the argument is not unduly loaded against either the older intellectual community or the radical students.

The young do not have a full-blown theory by which to situate their own position over against alternatives. They arrive upon the scene when there seems to be a vast consensus, a tradition that has been being appropriated with growing extension and solidarity since at least the first days of the New Deal. That tradition is anti-metaphysical; it values com-

3. Sponsored by the Freedom House Public Affairs Institute; see text in *The New York Times* (December 20, 1967).
4. "The Liberal War," vol. 87, no. 12, 350–351.
5. See Richard H. Rovere, *Waist Deep in the Big Muddy, op. cit.*

promise and adjustment; it prides itself upon its diagnosis of "real" interests and its estimate of immediate "realizable" possibilities; it thinks itself, in a word, unusually "realistic." As the young see it, however, this tradition has been operating with a social and political vision that has been reduced to automatic and trivial sequence. It is tired, repetitive in tactics and strategy, and increasingly out of contact with the dynamic energies of our time. The pragmatic tradition misread the conditions that resulted in the war in Vietnam and the conditions of despair and pride in the black community. Moreover, pragmatists seem blind to the fact that they, too, are ideologues. They neither defend nor criticize their own presuppositions, value judgments, predilected standards (like quantification), and political biases. They have tried so hard to be "objective" that they have failed to examine their own subjectivity—including economic status and professional commitments—for sources of distortion. Because mathematics is "objective" many think they are.

The students spot plenty of distortion. An occasional paper of the Center for the Study of Democratic Institutions, *Students and Society*[6] for example, offers unusually clear student testimony on this point. The word for professors is "technocrat." The American intellectual community seems to prefer "how to" questions, questions of prediction and control. Such questions demand as much quantification as the material will bear ("and then some"). Effectively, this preference removes the intellectual community from facing value questions and questions of ends—these are "soft" questions, and those who deal with them are considered unprofessional. Rewards go to hard-nosed analysts who provide the power of prediction and control.[7]

6. I, no. 1 (1967).
7. For further discussion, see Richard Lichtman, "The University: Mask for Privilege?", *The Center Magazine*, I, no. 2 (January 1968), 2–17 (including responses by Paul Goodman, Michael Harrington, Clark Kerr, Leo McLaughlin, and Rosemary Park); Theodore Roszak, "The Complacencies of the Academy," *The New American Review*, I, n. 1

Many professors do not seem sensitive to what their students are thinking or feeling; many would be surprised to think that, precisely as professors, they ought to be. Concentration is upon "objective" materials. Much worse, the limits of reality, for academic purposes, are established by professional circles in each discipline; what is important to such a circle is important, what is irrelevant to it does not, professionally, exist. The gap between the professional disciplines and the real world—where "real" means of concern to living human beings—could grow to great lengths before professionals would notice. But students have noticed. And to them specialization seems to be an escape from responsibilities as a human being. Professors perform their professional tasks, and then retreat to their comfortable upper middle class homes and private lives, like kept women of the American way of life. Their dignified phrases about truth and academic freedom could be claimed just as well by auto repairmen.

The close ties between major universities and the new technological industries, moreover, and the new dependence of state and national governments upon academic research and advice, have changed the role and character of the universities in society. In a rough way, the university is to our society what the Church used to be: its spiritual center, its source of guidance and legitimation. Its duly ordained experts are the clergymen of the new era: Walt H. Rostow as *éminence grise*. We have not yet devised ways of guaranteeing the separation of university and state.

Radical students turn upon their professors as Protestant reformers upon complacent and powerful medieval churchmen. The note of disappointed innocence is poignant: how *could* you, *you* above all? The one hope of cutting through the American myths of cherry pie, virginity, self-reliance, anti-communism,

---

(1967), 82–107; and Noam Chomsky, "The Responsibility of Intellectuals," *The New York Review of Books,* (VIII, n. 3).

crusades for freedom, and hard work lies in the university. Yet university professors appear to prefer the comfort of their sinecures to preaching the original revolutionary message of our land, the message transmitted through our Bill of Rights, our Constitution, the Statue of Liberty's call to the oppressed and poor of the world.

It is important to make clear that the protest of the reformers is not merely a protest of activists against theoreticians. The student Protestants are saying the the old *doctrines* are wrong, the theories are inadequate, the professors are blind to too many realities of life. The reformation is theoretical as well as practical. We have to revise our *conception* of knowledge and the role of science, our *view* of ourselves and of our world. The issues involved, in fact, sound like metaphysical or theological issues.

The students, however, have been well taught by pragmatic teachers; they do not know how to raise metaphysical questions; they retreat, instead, to gut reactions, They look at the war, the ghettoes, the increasing reaction of right-wing and liberal forces of "law and order," and they *feel* indignation. The corruption riven through American life by the interests of the comfortable is so palpable they can taste it and smell it. "All you have to do is open your eyes, man. If it don't make you sick, ain't nothin' no one can do for you." When one young man loses his bitterness—the center upon which he now pivots his personality—he pulls out a wrinkled photograph of babies disfigured by napalm[8]: his Spanish Jesus mutilated on the cross. Among the students there is an unmentioned litmus test: they study you to see if you feel what they feel. Liberals who talk "realistically" and "pragmatically," radicals believe, cannot possibly feel what their words imply: they know not what they do.

Yet the young are trapped. They reject the technocrats

8. *Students and Society, op. cit.,* p. 61.

but have pitifully few intellectual alternatives. When John Dewey and other great architects of the current pragmatic realism were teaching, they at least carried with them, implicitly but powerfully, the humanist tradition of their own earlier schooling; they advised their students, however, not to bother with the old masters of pre-scientific era. Some among the second generation of behavioral scientists, political scientists, social scientists, and analytical humanists, consequently, speak only one intellectual language. In rejecting that language, the present generation of students finds itself mute about its most urgent feelings. They do not *wish* to be anti-intellectual, but the one available intellectual language is abhorrent to them. Moreover, it is impossible for them to return to the classics, the great books, or the humanists—the recovery of a tradition that has now lapsed would turn them into historians, whereas it is the present and the future they most want to absorb and to comprehend. Had they the language, one feels, many of them would like to articulate clearly what is happening now, and thus produce new classics expressing our own cultural era. Mute instead, they can only say that those over thirty don't understand.

And surely they are right in feeling in their bones a new culture coming to birth. They need a vision of man adequate to the new time, and a political and social theory adequate to that vision. It ill becomes the older generation, which (overburdened by vast wars) has since 1932 provided so little by way of long-range vision or creative political and social theory, to demand that the students produce the longed-for vision and program in one stroke: instant ideology. The radical students need help. Specifically, they need fresh theories, new intellectual tools, openness to breakthroughs and readiness for originality. In many cases, all they need is someone to help them to articulate what they have already experienced and cannot quite say.

Thus, for example, the radicals speak in indignant tones of

87

corruption, sickness, and selling out; but they do not really mean to say that they think of themselves as pure, or that total purity of motive and conscience is possible for a human being. The vision of man which they seek must be utopian in the sense that it is an alternative to the present series of pragmatic adjustments and gives promise of a new cultural epoch. It need not be utopian in the sense that it represents a naïve innocence about man. Reflecting on the first five or six years of the movement, the radicals have learned that you can't trust anyone *under* thirty, either: not even yourself.

The radicals recognize that the rugged individualism of Ayn Rand, the inner-directed personality sketched by David Riesman, and the rational, atomic individual imagined by John Stuart Mill and the English empirical tradition are not now (if they ever were) viable models of human behavior. The social sciences—and political events—have taught them too well that the supposedly private, autonomous world of the self is in fact conditioned and shaped by the institutions in which human beings live, move, and have their being. The sense of reality is, itself, a social product.[9] Consequently, the radicals aspire to political consciousness in a proper sense: to become conscious of one's own identity is to become aware of institutional power already at work in oneself. The road to personal liberation is not private or through meditation, but political. Awareness grows through conscious, reflective, accurate action. The separation between thought and action, which present university life enforces, seems to the students illegitimate; and they argue the case on theoretical grounds.

The students seek fresh theories at many crucial places in the analysis of social reality. For example, when older liberals speak of "academic freedom and academic decorum" in connection with recent demontrations on campuses, they are

9. See Peter L. Berger and Thomas Luckmann, *The Social Construction of Reality* (New York, 1966).

thinking of McCarthyism, loyalty oaths, and the disruptive techniques of the Nazis in the 1920's. But the students are thinking of the enormous power of television and newspapers to establish the mainstream of public discourse. They see clearly how the honeyed discourse of public officials—which is ordinarily reported straight—instantly smothers the imaginations and emotions of all within their reach, and how a sweet coating is put upon all intentions and actions of the United States. The inherent respectability of official sources gains a multiplied, overwhelming power, and the entire burden of counter argument, unmasking, and reporting of contradictory interpretations passes over onto the few who are equipped for it. Commonly, the mass media cannot follow the subtleties of argument; moreover, officials merely announce; dissenters must document. Thus, a time lag of days, weeks, or months may be required before a rebuttal can be published. Worse, the very structure of the mass media makes dissenters seem querulous, nitpicking, obsessed; officials are encouraged to pose as noble and long-suffering.

The balance of power in the formation of public opinion has been altered by the advent of television. The society of independent, rational individuals envisaged by John Stuart Mill does not exist. The fate of all is bound up with the interpretation of events given by the mass media, by the image projected, and by the political power which results. The few with access to further information cannot compete with the many. Moreover, it is not so much "further information" that is at stake; it is the "image," the symbolic presentation of values, presuppositions, angle of vision, frame of reference, that is established by the media. In a society with respect for its political institutions, officials have only to act with decorum and energy in order to benefit by such respect and to have their views established as true until proven false.

Thus people are at the mercy of their government in a new and frightening way. The forces of "law and order"—army and police—are so powerful in the United States that no conceivable challenge could be raised against them. The technological society demands unity and thus the whole apparatus is concentrated in an awesome way in the hands of the federal government. "Freedom of speech," therefore, can no longer be governed merely by standards of decorum. The assumption that officials are speaking the truth can no longer be safely entertained by those who value their liberty. The credibility gap is not due to the personality of President Johnson; it now inheres in the office and in all public offices.

What, then, does freedom of speech mean in a technological society? How can one defend oneself against McCarthyism on the one hand, and official newspeak on the other? The solution of the students has been to violate the taboos of decorum and thus embrace Vice President Humphrey, the CIA, Dow Chemical and other enemies in an ugly scene, hoping that the unpopularity of the radicals will rub off on those embraced. They want to make the heretofore bland and respectable wear that tag which most alarms American sensibilities: "controversial."

This tactic suggests that it would be an advance in academic freedom never to allow a public official to share the privileges of academic discourse, unless followed immediately by a devil's advocate in open debate. We desperately need protection against our government, its agencies, and its industrial allies. We desperately need a theory of free speech and tolerance which takes account of advances in technology, in expanded population, and in industrial wealth and power. We need defense against the owners, advertisers, and official users of the mass media, and against those who rely upon traditional decorum and the need for law and order to make effective public challenge impossible. Given television and affluence, a government no longer needs a brazen Gestapo; it can win acquiescence by granting bread and circuses and announcing noble sentiments.

90

Thus many seeds of immense theoretical importance are germinating in the consciousness of the young. Never was it so clear that the role of the teacher—and today of the publicist—is as Plato described it: that of a midwife. Professors are not the fathers of the new consciousness, they are only midwives, looking on with alert and critical wonder at what the young, seeded who knows how or where, bring forth.

6. The Beauty of Earth

We seek a revolution in consciousness—a religious task. Yet
for many college students in America, talk about Christian
faith has been hopelessly compromised by unpleasant experiences with organized religion. A "religionless Christianity"
often seems to them just as irrelevant as a "religious" Christianity. On the other hand, many of the brightest students have
had experiences which they find it difficult to speak of in the
categories of pragmatism and science. With each year that
passes they are becoming more open to religious discourse.
Nevertheless, for various reasons they reject the language of
American Christianity and Judaism. In this context I would
like to argue that certain human experiences are ordinarily
prerequisite for an understanding of Christianity and, further,
that one malaise in contemporary Christian theology is due to
inattention to certain kinds of human experience. Consequently, I wish to argue for a greater openness to the lessons
of nature, a greater responsiveness to actual human experience,
apart from any reference to Christianity. Christians do not
need more Christianity, but less; Christians need a greater
openness to nature.

1. The Importance of Nature

Let me begin by citing four exceedingly important movements. (1) Probably the most significant development in the
contemporary religious world is the growing attraction which
Eastern and other world religions are beginning to exert upon

the consciousness of Christian nations. (2) The hippie culture of California is becoming a prototype of non-pragmatic experience for an increasing number of young people. (3) The often destructive use of psychedelic drugs does provide new experience, which cries out for expression in religious language. (4) The growing emphasis placed upon myth and symbol by contemporary sociology, psychology, and anthropology seems to signify the end of the Protestant, rationalistic, pragmatic, and scholastic era. These four movements are all interrelated. No doubt they depend upon the affluence and electronic technology of the present period. They mark, I believe, the beginning of a new age in the history of religion. They may be characterized by the reëmergence of the category of "nature" in human consciousness. A study of the work of a man who received the Nobel prize for illuminating the conscience of our time may make this point plain.

No writer is so widely read and so profoundly cherished by Amercian young people as Albert Camus. Yet one aspect of Camus' writing which critics have consistently overlooked, an aspect indispensable for understanding the contemporary consciousness, is his turning away from the Christian man of northern Europe to his "Mediterranean man," the man of the noonday sun.[1] Many writers interpret the modern period as a conflict between secularity and Christianity, between the German secular discovery of "historical consciousness" with its ideology of "the future" and more static Christian political and philosophical concepts. Camus reads modern history in a different light: "The profound conflict of this century is perhaps not so much between the German ideologies of history and Christian political concepts, which in a certain way are accomplices, as between German dreams and Mediterranean traditions . . .—in other words, between history and nature."[2] Camus links together Germanic devotion to the future and

1. See " 'Greece in Rags' and the Young Barbarians," in Parker's *Albert Camus: The Artist in the Arena,* pp. 25–45.
2. *The Rebel,* p. 299.

Christianity. He regrets the loss of Hellenism and its respect for nature, its view of man as an organic fruit of nature, a child of earth. "When nature ceases to be an object of contemplation and admiration, it can then be nothing more than material for an action that aims at transforming it."[3] Camus understood very well the lesson John Updike has drawn from the most future-oriented of all countries, the United States: "We in America have from the beginning been cleaving and baring the earth, attacking, reforming the enormity of nature we were given, which we took to be hostile. We have explored, on behalf of all mankind, this paradox: the more matter is outwardly mastered, the more it overwhelms us in our hearts."[4] In brief, Camus' diagnosis of our illness is precisely the opposite of those who ask Christianity to take on an even more one-sided orientation toward the future. For Camus, we have drunk too much history and have repressed nature.

Let us dwell on Camus' analysis a little longer—it is a point he made in his *Notebooks*, in the *Myth of Sisyphus*, and also in the *Rebel*. Camus used the phrase "German ideology" to refer to "the violence of eternal adolescence," "romanticism," a "nostaligia rendered more acute by knowledge and by books." "Despite its pretensions," he says, "it begins in the absolute and attempts to mold reality." It uses the future as a lever against the present. By contrast, "rebellion" is grounded in "Mediterranean traditions," in "virile strength," in "courage reinforced and enlightened by the experience of life," and "it relies primarily on the most concrete realities."[5] In this contest between history and nature, German ideology, he writes,

has come into an inheritance. It consummates twenty centuries of abortive struggle against nature, first in the name of a historic god and then of a deified history. Christianity, no doubt, was only able

3. *Ibid.*
4. *Pigeon Feathers and Other Stories* (New York, 1962), p. 248.
5. *The Rebel*, pp. 289–299.

to conquer its catholicity by assimilating as much as it could of Greek thought. But when the Church dissipated its Mediterranean heritage, it placed the emphasis on history to the detriment of nature, caused the Gothic to triumph over the romance, and, destroying a limit in itself, has made increasing claims to temporal power and historical dynamism. When nature ceases to be an object of contemplation and admiration, it can then be nothing more than material for an action that aims at transforming it. These tendencies—and not the concepts of mediation, which would have comprised the real strength of Christianity—are triumphing in modern times, to the detriment of Christianity itself, by an inevitable turn of events. That God should, in fact, be expelled from this historical universe and German ideology be born where action is no longer a process of perfection but pure conquest, is an expression of tyranny.[6]

The source of the death of God, for Camus, does not lie in the use of the Hellenic category of "being," nor in any of those other places where theologians whose nourishment comes from northern European sources divine it. God dies because man has been uprooted from nature, historicized, and rendered a tyrant over and an alien in his own environment. Yet there is, Camus senses,

an irrepressible demand of human nature, of which the Mediterranean, where intelligence is intimately related to the blinding light of the sun, guards the secret. . . . In the common condition of misery, the eternal demand is heard again; nature once more takes up the fight against history. Naturally, it is not a question of despising anything, or of exalting one civilization at the expense of another, but of simply saying that it is a thought which the world today cannot do without for very much longer.[7]

Camus, of course, is not interested in rehabilitating the notion of God, only in making human life more possible for man. He finds it humiliating that for twenty centuries the

6. *Ibid.*, pp. 299–300.
7. *Ibid.*

West has had a Christian image of man. "Who can say what we should be if those twenty centuries had clung to the ancient ideal with its beautiful fate?"[8] Camus has hold here of something extremely important—the vitality and the power of man's biological life. How shall we ever regain our sanity as a culture unless we become reconciled to our body? Man is not, in the phrase of Alan Watts, an ego trapped in a bag of skin, alien to his environment. Man is a part of nature, brought forth from the universe like fruit from a tree. The universe is a *thou* to him, inseparable from his own self, part of him, and he is in dialogue with it. As an apple tree *apples*, so the universe *peoples*—if again we may use a phrase of Alan Watts'.

Thus Camus saw with joy and urgency the need for a return to nature. He saw the need for a return to nudity and simple delight in the beauty of the flesh.

For the first time in two thousand years the body has appeared naked on beaches. For twenty centuries men have striven to give decency to Greek insolence and naïveté, to diminish the flesh and complicate dress. Today, despite that history, young men running on Mediterranean beaches repeat the gestures of the athletes of Delos. And living thus among bodies and through one's body, one becomes aware that it has . . . a psychology of its own. The body's evolution, like that of the mind, has its history, its vicissitudes, its progress, and, . . . its deficiency. . . . How can one fail to participate, then, in that dialogue of stone and flesh in tune with the sun and seasons?[9]

One senses in California today, as in Algeria so loved by Camus, the burgeoning renewed trust in the human body. One finds young people, as it were, trying to put Humpty-Dumpty together again, beginning with the things closest to them, the things that their hands can touch, learning the meaning of community, dignity, sadness, joy.

8. *Notebooks 1942–1951* (New York, 1966), p. 8.
9. *The Myth of Sisyphus* (New York, 1955), p. 106.

I have the mad hope that, without knowing it perhaps, these barbarians lounging on beaches are actually modeling the image of a culture in which the greatness of man will at last find its true likeness. This race, wholly cast into its present, lives without myths, without solace. It has put all its possessions on this earth and therefore remains without defense against death. All the gifts of physical beauty have been lavished on it. . . . And yet, yes, one can find measure as well as excess in the violent and keen face of this race. . . . Between this sky and these faces turned toward it, nothing on which to hang a mythology, a literature, an ethic, or a religion, but stones, flesh, stars, and those truths the hand can touch.[10]

There is something of penetrating beauty in this natural return to paganism, this wholehearted sense of nature in its measure and its limitations.

At a time when doctrinaire attitudes would separate us from the world, it is well for young men in a young land to proclaim their attachment to those few essential and perishable possessions that give meaning to our lives: the sun, the sea and women in the sunlight. They are the riches of the living culture, everything else being the dead civilization that we repudiate. If it is true that true culture is inseparable from a certain barbarianism, nothing that is barbaric can be alien to us.[11]

Moreover, Camus sees in this modest sense of nature the solid base of a revolutionary ethic. He well realized that within a few miles of the beaches of Algeria on which his maroon athletes lounged, there were villages where people, scabbed with various diseases, starved to death. Camus wished to find a way of wedding political consciousness to respect for nature. He found this way in his concept of rebellion. The Greek myth of Nemesis guided his thought here, as the myth of Sisyphus had earlier. "The revolutionary mind, if it wants to

10. *Ibid.*, p. 111.
11. "Presentation de la revue 'Rivages'," *Rivages,* No. 1 (1939), 1, as quoted by Parker in *Albert Camus*, pp. 40–41.

remain alive, must therefore return again to the sources of rebellion and draw its inspiration from the only system of thought which is faithful to its origin: thought that recognizes limits. . . . Rebellion, at the same time that it suggests a nature common to all men, brings to light the measures and the limit which are the very principle of this nature."[12]

He wrote further:

Analysis of rebellion leads at least to the suspicion that, contrary to the postulates of contemporary thought, a human nature does exist, as the Greeks believed. Why rebel if there is nothing permanent in oneself worth preserving? . . . The slave asserts himself when he comes to the conclusion that a command has infringed on something in him which . . . is common ground where all men—even the man who insults and oppresses him—have a natural community. . . . From this point of view human solidarity is metaphysical.[13]

For Camus, in short, the rebel rejects and disputes history in the name of nature. Camus does not deny that man is responsible for history. He only wishes to make plain that man is part of nature. Man may possibly be "evolution become conscious of itself," but Camus wishes us to be certain that we do not become conscious in an alienated, rootless, unnatural way. Nature lives in us, and we in it. Nature is historical, and history natural. To wave a banner *either* in the name of history against nature *or* of nature against history is to misunderstand our own identity.

For some time the entire effort of our philosophers has aimed solely at replacing the notion of human nature with that of situation, and replacing ancient harmony with the disorderly advance of chance or reason's pitiless progress. . . . Nature is still there, however. She contrasts her calm skies and her reason with the madness of men. Until the atom too catches fire and history ends

12. *The Rebel*, p. 294.
13. *Ibid.*, pp. 16–17.

in the triumph of reason and the agony of the species. But the Greeks never said that the limit could not be overstepped. They said it existed and whoever dared to exceed it was mercilessly struck down. Nothing in present history can contradict them.[14]

2. In Defense of Religion

What is the bearing of the new paganism of Camus upon the problem of God? It suggests that the problem of God is not to be solved by seeking a "religionless Christianity," but by a move in quite the opposite direction. We might say that Christianity has been weakened because it has had too high a component of "Christianity," and because its component of "religion" has been exhausted. Christianity may be a good seed; but it cannot thrive in thin, sandy, or rocky soil. It is religion which makes the human heart fertile. We need more religion and less Christianity.

"The Greek myths," I have recently heard a student say, "speak much more powerfully to me than Christian myths." Another student wrote in his term paper: "Christian stories never impressed my imagination so vividly as stories of the American Indian gods: tales of thunder and the Presence in the mighty rivers. It was in *those* stories that I first understood the meaning of 'God,' which I later lost in Christian education." Herman Hesse's *Siddhartha* startles many students into awareness, and the wisdom of the East begins to speak directly to their hearts.[15] Why is this? I believe that Camus' theory is correct. German ideology—its emphasis on man's future projects—rests upon too cerebral, too egoistical and too tyrannical a view of man. The organic, biological, and imaginative life of Americans and other future-oriented people has been starved. "God" has not died because the Hellenic con-

14. *The Myth of Sisyphus,* pp. 136–137.
15. See, for example, Alan Watts, *The Way of Zen* (New York, 1957).

cept of being was used to speak of him. "God" has died because the word "being" has lost its roots in human biology, human experience, and human imagination. The great, profound *Om* which Siddhartha labored long to find deep in the pit of his stomach says much more adequately what "being" used to say. We do not need to dehellenize the word "God." We need to turn to nature and myth as the Greeks did, in order to give human depth to our faith.

There is, of course, an ambiguity in the word "religion." When Bonhoeffer attacked "religion," he attacked a widespread kind of inwardness, separateness, artificialty—a piety which led religious people out of the center of life.[16] But why did religion do that? Because religion had lost its roots in nature—lost its roots in sea, wind, the nudity of beautiful human beings, sunlight on beautiful women, courage, political consciousness. It may clarify matters to recall that just as Bonhoeffer was working out his vision of a religionless Christianity, Camus was working out his vision of secular sanctity. The basic momentum in both arguments is to turn men toward the center of life—toward the kiss of lovers, the coolness of the evening air, the demand today for quiet courage in rebellion against the manipulators of the future.

It is because Americans dread the public use of four-letter words, insist on cleanliness and neatness, think human genitals are dirty, fear controversy, will not admit drinking and gambling into public life, refuse to imagine that their leaders could ever lie or use power tyrannically or kill innocent people—it is because Americans try in the name of "religion" to cover up reality that "religion" has atrophied and God has died. Christianity without raw nature, Christianity without reality, is the *Logos* who never became flesh. Genuine religion, honest religion, is the flesh which the Word assumes, the soil in which the seed is sown.

Thus the tack taken by those who follow uncritically in the

16. *Letters and Papers from Prison* (New York, 1953), pp. 162–166.

path of Bonhoeffer is, I believe, a mistaken and sterile one. If there is no God, the figure of Jesus is without interest. So long as we do not turn to nature, there can be no God. But how, we are certain to be asked, does turning to nature lead us to God?

3. *The God Within*

A series of insights or orientations is needed if an American is to discover God in his own experience. For example, an American student will commonly imagine that "turning to nature" means turning to objects "out there" in the environment. The ordinary American student has been taught to think of himself as a center of consciousness imprisoned subjectively in a sheeting of thin flesh and confronted with an environment full of objects out there to be observed objectively and mastered. In brief, the American has been taught to view the universe as made up of two kinds of stuff, conscious and unconscious, of which the first is an alien, an intruder, an outsider. It comes as a surprise to many to recognize that this "myth of the objective observer" is in fact a myth, and that they are free to look at themselves in a quite different way, living as organically in their environment as an apple lives on a tree. Nature courses through them and shares its consciousness with them. They are free to feel "at one" with nature. They may speak to nature as to themselves. They may imagine that the imaginative form for presenting their relationship to the ocean, to trees, to buildings, to chairs, to desks is not the form "it" but the form "thou." Consciousness, intelligibility, presence—we fumble for the telling word—pervades all things. "*Tat tvam asi:* That art Thou." Thus does the famous Hindu expression articulate the identity of the soul and God, an identity whose presence extends to every moment and to every place.

It is important, I would argue, for Westerners to begin to

101

recover ancient experiences of man's relation to the world and of men's relations to one another. It is not true that metaphysics is at an end; it is only at a beginning. The functional patterns of scientific thinking have their place; they serve the purposes of prediction and control, so that man is able to extend the power of his aims and purposes over his environment. But the logic of science is the logic of tyranny: as Francis Bacon saw, scientific knowledge is power. The scientific model for action is the manipulation of objects. Scientific thinking applied to metaphysical questions destroys metaphysics.

However, the expansion of scientific information and its extension through technology is bringing about a major correction in the assumptions of recent generations. Questions about nature and about man's nature are regaining their primacy in the most technologically advanced nations. As men begin to take responsibility for building the urban centers of the future, they are forced to ask the questions: "What sort of cities do we desire? What forms best realize human potential? Who do we think we are?" Anthropological and sociological societies have discovered in recent years that while their methods may in some sense be value free, their employment on real human beings has empirical, social effects and hence involve investigators in serious value commitments. Among engineers who dream not only of the constructs which will be operational in a few years, but of those not yet realized even in design, the fundamental question is: "*Should* we do X? By what values should we decide which X's to do?"

In brief, what Aristotle called architectonic questions of politics and ethics are beginning to dominate human consciousness. And the mysteries of the human self, the multiplicity of future possibilities, and an almost universal identity crisis are reasserting their primacy. The fundamental question for the children of an affluent society, trained to technical skills, is: *Who are we? What do we wish to do with ourselves, and with our power?*

A second series of insights emerges when students try to answer the question, *Who am I?* If they keep a diary, or attempt to write out who they think they are and what they think their values are, they speedily discover that what they commit to paper one day seems woefully inadequate the next. The self is elusive. Its values and sense of identity refuse to be condensed in words. In answering the Socratic question, they begin to understand the point of the Socratic method. Knowledge is not power; it is knowledge of ignorance. Moreover, the self is inextricably and organically linked to its environment and to its societies. The question "Who am I?" launches a dialectic that leads to discoveries about one's economic, social, political, mythical, and biological history. The Hindu insight, *"Tat tvam asi:* That art Thou," is verified in greater richness than one had at first anticipated.

Thirdly, it is commonly impossible for young Americans to deal with the Socratic question or with the question of God unless they have first shared the experience of communion with at least one other person. This experience, for young Americans, is more rare than one might expect. There has perhaps never been a generation for whom the sense of loneliness is so acute. Their parents, after a fashion, love them, but the family is no longer, nor can it be, the nest it used to be. Moreover, young people have been taught that other people are their competitors, objects whose friendship and influence they must try to win. Achievement is rewarded. Popularity and acceptability are established as criteria for human relations. The Beatles comment accurately: "She's leaving home/ After living alone for so many years." It is not unusual for college students, suddenly aware of one another, to fall into one another's arms, to hug one another tightly, and to cry both from fear and from joy. Many young people from "good middle-class homes" have never known the sense of community with another human being. They are "uptight" about touching one another.

Moreover, Christian society in America has publicly treated

the human genitals as organs of embarrassment and shame, the *pudenda*. Consequently, the genital organs are surrounded by taboos; "breasts," "nipples," and "penis" are suppressed words, and the actions of lovemaking are thought to be "obscene." Nevertheless, the mutual revelation of two people to each other gives rise to the most poignant sense of the sacred in our society. In sexual openness one "transcends" the stultifying mores of society; in intimacy and tenderness one "transcends" the acquisitive, impersonal human interchange of our society. For many persons it is only, or chiefly, in sexual love that one encounters the category of an end in itself, the category of the sacred. Everything else in our society appears to be a means; the commercialization of sexuality—and the common ecclesiastical view of sex—threaten to degrade even sexual love into a means. Yet for many of the young no human experience is more full of awe, joy, and holiness than sexual intercourse. It is from this experience, for many, that religious language becomes meaningful again. The honesty, community, and absolute respect for the other which good lovers are led to share takes them beyond the categories of the pragmatic, the rationalistic, and the isolated self.

Why is it, then, that Christian society tolerates violence and murders by the dozen in movies and on evening television, but outlaws manifestations of sexual love? Is it moral to strike a man in the face in a barroom brawl, but not to caress a woman's breasts? Is it clean to plunge a knife into a man again and again, but dirty for a man to enter into a woman with gentleness? Christian society has come to prefer repression of vital and sacred instincts, and has conceived of God as the transcendent, all-seeing Eye who detects every violation of sexual taboos. The God of American Christianity has been the idol of inhibition, repression, and shame. The death of this God should have been predictable.

Conventional American society, in short, has been hostile to every basic human experience from which language about God commonly springs. If conventional American society is "religious," then by all means we need a "religionless Christianity." Yet I have been trying to suggest that American society is not genuinely religious; it is self-contained, repressive, uncritical, and idolatrous. The question which remains to be answered is why the experiences of nature, the self, community, and sexual love lead many young Americans to a religious language. Why do these experiences constantly break through the ordinary patterns of life and establish the sacred in the midst of man's strength?

Perhaps the best way to understand the emergence of religious categories is to grasp the character of technological, pragmatic life in advanced countries like the United States. From the perspective of studies in Marx and Freud, Herbert Marcuse in *One Dimensional Man* has come to describe such life as effectively totalitarian; people think that they are free, but they are only free within the limits established by the pragmatic consensus. Technical society awakens false needs and false consciousness; it is virtually impossible not to be inwardly determined by such needs and such consciousness, much more so than at earlier stages of man's development. M. Garaudy, the famed Marxist interpreter of Christianity, continually assaults Christianity for its "inwardness" and "subjectivity."[17] Christian critics, unfortunately, appear to concede too much to Garaudy on this point. For it is the strength of Christianity and the weakness of Marxism that the criteria of humanistic life are centered in the human person and the critical community, not in the impersonal processes of technical, pragmatic life. On the other hand, the inwardness of existentialism and of Christianity is by no means contained within the private sphere. Sartre and Camus possess an acute social and political consciousness; there is an existentialist politics.[18]

The heart of existentialist politics, in fact, lies in its rejection

17. See, for example, "Christian-Marxist Dialogue," *Journal of Ecumenical Studies,* IV (1967), 207–222.
18. See Michel-Antoine Burnier, *Choice of Action* (New York, 1968).

of the presuppositions of the present technical consensus, which it judges to be inhuman and irrational. It is not a mistake in government, nor the fault of any one administration, that the United States and Russia spend so many billions of dollars for destructive armaments. The irrationality of the Cold War springs from the dominance of pragmatic and technical considerations over a radical humanistic critique of the system under which the secular city is being built. Consequently, it appears to be a mistake for Harvey Cox and Johannes B. Metz to surrender the strength of subjectivity and inwardness because of Marxist objections.[19] A certain kind of private inwardness is pale and sickly, to be sure, an interior life oblivious to the power of institutions and economic structures and irresponsible in social and political affairs. A great many sins of this sort have been committed by Christians.

The cure for sickly inwardness, however, is not pragmatism, nor a zest for technique, nor devotion to the future of man. The cure for sickly inwardness is a conversion to social and political responsibility. But *why* should a man be concerned about other men? Why should he become involved? The history of our time seems to indicate that political life is murderous and that society is impervious to intelligence and courage. The great leap of faith is faith in man. One must, despite appearances, trust in the power of critical intelligence, courage, and compassion. One must, despite odds, go on struggling for a more brotherly city. Solace between individuals is not enough; community structures must be changed. A reconstruction of the economic, social, and political order is called for if men are to develop into men.

Thus openness to nature, to the Socratic question, to the experience of community, and to sexual love become *models* for what it is to be a man, and *sources* of faith in man. It is only

19. See *The Secular City* (New York, 1967); *Journal of Ecumenical Studies*, IV (1967), 223–234.

when persons become awakened from their sleep and recognize that the assumptions of a technical, pragmatic society have blinded them to their inner possibilities that hope for a political revolution can be generated. The awareness of the mystery of the self and the mystery of community becomes the criterion by which social, economic, and political realities are judged: do they stultify or do they stimulate this awareness?

But to become aware of the mystery of the self and of the mystery of communion with others is to gain a sense of "participation" and of "unity," a sense of being part of something in which one does not lose one's own identity but does lose one's alienation and isolation. In being honest, one has the sense of being honest *against oneself* and yet somehow in the name of oneself—not as if under the glare of an all-seeing Eye, but as if by "participating" in a light greater than one's own emotions, interests, or rationalizations. In loving another as other, one has the sense of responding outside the categories of subject and object, or interest, or need, or stimulus and response. In moments of courage one has the sense of surrendering the interests of the self, not exactly for an abstraction or even a value, but for a self more important than the interested self. From such experiences of honesty, community, and courage, religious language is bound to spring. Human life is not self-contained. Who has belief in man has already made the giant leap of faith, compared to which the leap to religious language is only a step. The sense of man as an end in himself suggests that the radical structure of the universe in which we live is not hostile nor even impersonal; those who treat men as ends in themselves seem to live most fittingly. Why is this so? One cannot help wondering. One may reject the repressive, transcendent "God" of false religiousness; but the wonder which is the ever-fecund source of true religion springs up like clear water in the heart. No one sees God. All that we encounter is the sense of human experience leading beyond pragmatic and technical categories, out of the area of means and ends. Here arises the sense of the sacred and the darkness of which the mystics wrote.

4. *Jesus Is Not Enough*

What are some of the fruits of turning to nature? Thomas J. J. Altizer has been telling us eloquently that the God of history is dead. Who is the God of history? He is the transcendent One, Providence, the Repressor, the Father. Altizer takes seriously the crisp affirmation: "God was in Jesus." The transcendent God "emptied himself," negated himself, becoming so immanent in history that the only legitimate way of speaking of him is through affirmations about Jesus. I believe that Altizer is making several most important points. But I think it is necessary to go beyond his position in two ways.

In the first place, Jesus is not, of himself, especially attractive. A man among other men, he suffers too many liabilities— too many innocents died on account of him, too many horrors have been for centuries committed in his name (upon Jews and Arabs, for example, but also upon the sexual and psychological life of countless Christians, too). Moreover, his own character and deeds are ambivalent; not all men are attracted to him, not all admire him in every respect.

In the second place, a common Protestant understanding of the transcendence of faith is—it seems to me—faulty. On this understanding, a man cannot come either to experience or to knowledge of God except through the historical, in-breaking grace of Jesus. Any knowledge of God at which man arrives through his own experience and understanding apart from Jesus is idolatrous. Yet we are told in the prologue of St. John's Gospel that in the beginning was the Word, and that all things were made through him. The vision behind this prologue seems to suggest that every person, thing, and event in history has been made in the image of the Word. We should expect, then, that every culture, every person, every moment of history reveals the creative presence of the Word. Thus the grace of the Word does not only break into history through the historical Jesus; *all* things have been made in him, through him, and with him. All things are graced—"Everything we look upon is blest" (Yeats). Thus, I think we must say that even the historical Jesus can be used idolatrously; that is to say, in a manner that overlooks the omnipresence and the efficacy of Jesus insofar as he is the Word by whom, through whom, and with whom were made all the things that were made. Nature itself is a word mirroring and echoing the Word. Like the castle of Albee's *Tiny Alice* it is a castle within a castle within a castle: its reverberating air shaped by a Word.

Thus Teilhard de Chardin is able to step with swift strides from evolutionary nature and the Omega Point to Jesus as the Word. Is not the Alpha also the Omega, and does not abyss cry out to abyss in glory? Teilhard de Chardin, like Dostoevsky and Berdyaev, drew his nourishment from Greek Christianity, which saw a dynamic universe flowing forth from the *Pantokrator*, the *Logos*, the *Risen Lord*. What has come to be despised in scholasticism as "Hellenization" is, in fact, "Latinization." It is Latin categories rather than Greek, based on commerce and jurisprudence rather than upon potent, dynamic nature, that have led to the death of the transcendent God.

In nature itself, the nature known to physical science and the nature known to ordinary human experience, there are, if Christianity be true, elements leading the reflective man to honesty rather than to dishonesty, to creativity rather than to destruction, to courage to be rather than to anomie, to community rather than to atomic isolation. The universe in which we live often seems impersonal, indifferent, hostile, and even cruel. Yet our experience within it often fills us with reconciliation, with a sense of unity and peace, with a profound stirring of ecstasy and the desire to create. The transcendent

109

is immanent in the world as yeast in dough, as powers of growth in a mustard seed, as shaping word in air. It is through nature as it is that God is to be found. Such a conviction is profoundly Oriental, profoundly Greek, and profoundly Christian. Who says the Buddha's *Om* says *Word*.[20]

What Christianity adds to Greek and to Oriental religions is a responsibility not only to reflect the world, but also to change it. Creation is unfinished; each man, in the image of the creative Word, must utter a creative word. But man was separated from his environment and history was separated from nature by the first cycle of modern science, by the printing press, and by Germanic eschatology. Modern science has entered a new cycle, the printing press has been replaced by electronic media, and now it is time to turn from Germanic eschatology[21] to Mediterranean nature. Camus refused to surrender the present moment to the future. Visions of the future must share time with the world of total present experience,

20. Nancy Wilson Ross, *Three Ways of Asian Wisdom* (New York, 1966), p. 24. Western men cannot simply accept Eastern religious themes, of course. Western experiences and Western questions must be accounted for. In order to experience the world as one, for example, it is not necessary to understand concrete realities as mere *maya*. What I mean to argue for is the interpenetration and mutual criticism of Eastern and Western concepts. A *coincidentia oppositorum* is necessary, if we are to experience an international wisdom in our time.

21. When completing this paper, I had not yet read Jürgen Moltmann's *Theology of Hope* (New York, 1967). There are powerful passages and useful distinctions in the book. The treatment of nature and present experience is inadequate—the restlessness and self-driving, self-expanding impulse are characteristically German and (I would say) dangerous. The treatment of Camus is only of the early Camus and far too facile. Moreover, although the argument of the book is carried out in theological words, its moving spring is quite clearly the cultural pressure arising from a new stage of science, technology, and international politics—a fresh perception of man's experience of his own present. Its key values like "more justly, more humanely, more peacefully, and in mutual recognition . . . of human dignity and freedom" (pp. 337–338) seem to have their ground in human experience not limited to Christians. In America, Babbitt was a "booster," there are Optimist Clubs, and hope is often a mask by which present horrors are evaded and the compulsion to master history, space, and matter is legitimized. Theology played on one string is not an orchestra.

experience of the senses, the imagination, the emotions, and the intelligence and will. Man is coming to life again; taste and see that the taste of life is sweet! When man regains his roots in nature, the God immanent in nature courses through his consciousness again. The dead God rises. The arrowhead breaks through into a new, creative, period.

7. Human First, Christian Second

"What does it mean to be a Christian?" As a theological theme, that question seems to be diminishing in importance. "What does it mean to be a human being?" That question grows in theological importance, and there are both empirical and theological reasons for this priority.

In principle, it seems good to attend more closely to our actual experience as Christians than to theories, formulas or doctrines which purport to articulate and to direct that experience. For experience is in principle richer, more complex, and more full of novelty than limited conceptual schemes can compass. Fresh attention to experience is a major source of newer and more accurate formulas. Of course, the relationship between experience and theory is reciprocal; theory points us in a direction, helps us to escape from unobservant and confined habits, often awakens us to the world around us. Theory, however, is for the sake of life, and sometimes the lure of life exceeds what present theories can handle. Ours seems to be such a time.

1.

We have been taught that there are great and obvious differences between the Christian and the unbelieving humanist. In our actual experience of life, it is difficult to detect these differences. Many who call themselves atheists or agnostics are, in the way they live and according to the values their lives affirm, indistinguishable from Christians. I am not trying to suggest that such people are "hidden Christians" or "Christians in disguise," but the contrary: good Christians may be nothing more than good human beings in disguise. Looking over my friends at a party or facing a classroom full of students, I find it hard to think up empirical tests by which one could distinguish which of them are atheists, which Christians. Many of the students who take religion courses are agnostics or atheists. As I read autobiographical essays in which the students describe the basic experiences and reflections which seem to them to reveal their own identity to themselves, I am repeatedly struck by the interchangeability of the inner life of Christians and atheists: I find no experience or method of reflection exclusively Christian or exclusively atheistic. Joy, alienation, darkness, peace, wonder, rebellion, reconciliation, guilt—the essays reveal a startling similarity in the range, depth and synthesis of fundamental human experiences and attitudes.

According to the theories we have inherited from the past, there *should* be differences between a Christian and an atheist. Otherwise, why bother to be a Christian or to become an atheist? In practice, however (at least in the United States), the differences are very difficult to detect and the similarities are overwhelming. I must agree with the thesis of Anthony Levi in *Religion in Practice*,[1]: that in our culture, from an empirical point of view, when you find a good Christian or a good Jew performing exactly as a good Christian or a good Jew ought to perform, his behavior is indistinguishable from the behavior of a good secular humanist.

Moreover, as I read with attention the works of writers— Albert Camus, Bertrand Russell, Walter Kaufmann, Sidney Hook, Jean-Paul Sartre, Gerhard Szczesny, *et al.*—who describe themselves as atheists or even as anti-Christian, I often

1. New York, 1966.

find in them the spiritual kinship that I find in some Christian writers but not in others; I feel closer to them than to many Christian theologians. When they list their objections against Christianity, their views of Jesus Christ and the characteristics of the God they reject, I more commonly find myself agreeing with them (from their standpoint) than disagreeing. When they state the values to which they give primary allegiance, I find myself making the same sort of appropriation—critical but grateful—as I make with Christian writers of comparable stature. These atheists often seem closer in their perceptions to various insights of the Gospels than some Christian theologians are.

In brief, the experiences of everyday living and everyday reflection seem to show that the same graces of understanding and loving which are touchstones of a Christian presence are manifested prodigally among those who are not Christians. Grace, wrote Georges Bernanos, is everywhere. Experience bears him out.

But there are also theological reasons for the proposition that becoming human is, for Christians, a prior matter to becoming Christian. In the first place, there is only one world —not both a natural world and a Christian world, but only one concrete world, this one. It is true that this world (from a Christian point of view) is made in, through and by the Word. It was conceived in the image of Jesus. And Jesus, the humble man of an underdeveloped land of the first century, is also the Lord who was before Abraham and before all the ages, the Alpha and the Omega. The Greek Christian tradition, it appears, has maintained the image of Jesus as Word, Lord, Pantokrator and, with it, the idea of the unity of the world, more adequately than Western Christianity has done. Western Christianity tends toward a dualism of the two orders, a dualism of creation and redemption, nature and supernature, natural religion and revelation, wordliness and grace.

Yet (from a Christian point of view) there is only one

world, the world made in the image of the Word. There is not now, there never was, there never will be a purely "natural" man. Naturalism is an abstraction. In the concrete, everything has been graced; nothing is merely profane, secular, natural. Every historical event, person and culture has been created in and through the Word, and by him also, yet more graciously, redeemed.

This one, concrete world of grace is also, of course, as both empirical experience and Christian tradition make plain, a world of contingency, dishonesty, betrayal, irrationality, tragedy, absurdity. The sign of Jesus is the surd: the cross, from which grace does not spare us. Redemption does not bring escape from absurdity, but reconciliation, the will to struggle, and continual new beginnings. Redemption does not save us from our own infidelities, inconsistencies, cruelties or conceits, which seem to continue without end. Christianity is not, in that sense, a religion of salvation; it is a religion of hard and painful reality.

2.

The world is as it is. Christianity does not wish us to picture it otherwise. Is it surprising, then, that the atheist may see what the world is like as clearly as the Christian, though he will not use the words "the fall," "hell," "redeemed," etc.? Is it surprising that the atheist sometimes even borrows Christian symbols to express his view of what the world is like? It is the same world that Christian and atheist share, made (if the Christian is right) in the image of the Word and distorted by the absurd and the malicious; fallen and redeemed. The psychologist and the sociologist whose respect for the complexity and intractability of their materials leads them to devise ever more subtle and flexible methods of inquiry will, we may expect, teach us as much about the meaning of personal identity, love, community, freedom and power as the most profound theologians have taught. The God who revealed himself in Jesus reveals himself also in the evolution of creation: in one Word both are said. The faithful novelist, in telling us what the world is like, speaks unawares of the Word.

We are living, as Teilhard de Chardin pointed out, in the noösphere; increasingly, men share the same consciousness. The "good news" of Jesus has been spread abroad, has been appropriated in countless ways in the scientific, social and political life of the world, and in many diverse ways in the personal lives of men. There are by now few men who have not been touched by the sources of life and value that Jesus sowed in history; the mustard tree has spread its roots and branches everywhere. To be sure, these realities are no longer always called by Christian names or expressed in theological concepts. They have taken on secular forms. It may be true that the present period is one of "secularization." But it seems also to be one in which the institutions of society are judged by the most universal application of Christian standards in history: the dignity of the lowly, compassion, dialogue, equality, truth, freedom, social justice, responsibility for the future. The movement may be described as one of secularization, but it may also be described as one in which atheists, agnostics and men of non-Christian religions embrace standards which Christianity helped to shape.

One cannot say, of course, that the Christian tradition is the sole source of modern humanism. Greek thought, the way of life of the Buddha, the rise of scientific humanism, the Enlightenment and the original intuitions of many atheists have brought us to the present. Yet (from a Christian point of view) all of history has been conceived in the image of the Word. The same Word speaks outside the Christian tradition as within it. Non-Christians know truths about this Word (though they do not employ his name) that Christians have yet to learn. It is not true that Christians know all that is to be learned about Jesus or about human destiny. For not everything that is to be learned about the Word will be known until history, conceived in his image, shall be complete.

There is only one world: the point cannot be emphasized too strongly. It is a world of truth and untruth, grace and absurdity, destruction and creativity, evil and beauty. Christians and others share in all aspects of it. The same battles rage in the hearts of all. None is simply pure.

Radical theologians, it sometimes seems, confuse us on this point by employing the criteria and methods of secular inquiry, on the one hand, and biblical and Christian concepts, on the other. Their procedure leads many Christians to think that such theologians are amputating Christianity in order to make it conform to the present spirit of the age. By contrast, it leads secular men to think that the radical theologians are not genuinely secular—for the secular man sees no point in the biblical and Christian superstructure such theologians seem to impose upon secularization. Even Bonhoeffer does not escape this charge.

3.

My proposal is a little different. It is in opposition to Barth, even the later Barth; yet it does not return to Schleiermacher and liberalism. I wish to say that Christians must look freshly and critically at the new events and movements of every age, because the Word is expressed, although ambiguously, in the complexities of history. Jesus is already present in history—his presence is not confined within the bounds of the covenanted community. It is an error to set world over against church, secular thought over against Christian theology, man over against God. Grace is everywhere, and the Holy Spirit blows where he wills. No concrete person, event, movement of culture is merely secular. Christ is alive everywhere in human history, if we have eyes to see.

There is no need, of course, to justify secular events by the

117

presence of Christ in them or to justify secularization as biblical. It is just the opposite that I wish to stress. There is only one world. By the fact that anything is, it is already good, already gracious, already redeemed. We need not speak about it in theological or Christian terms. The Christian tradition, its language and its methods are, in fact, too narrow and parochial. A Christian ought to feel free to speak in a new, secular way about his values, attitudes and beliefs, without always trying to make his speech fit into older molds. At the same time, he can remain confident that the Word is somehow expressed by every historical event. Moreover, he may feel entitled to seek out connections between what he learns afresh from the Word through historical events and what he has been taught about Jesus within the church. For Jesus is the Word; the source is one and the same. The comparatively narrow tradition of the Christian church needs to be expanded, and the ambiguities of history need to be discerned and interpreted.

There is, in short, a dialectic between the two locations of our knowledge about the Word. On some occasions, new discoveries from history lead us to interpret afresh the Jesus of the church. On other occasions, new reflection upon the Jesus of the church teaches us to discern heretofore unnoticed aspects of historical movements and events. The Christian is one who lives between both sources of stimulation. He is also, of course, twice as liable to err—to become either too churchy, or else too indiscriminate in his acceptance of history.

Even Bonhoeffer, it appears, despite his intention to open himself to atheists and to secular society, was too confident that the pattern for that society was already known to the church, already known in Jesus. As he put it:

The world's coming of age is then no longer an occasion for polemics and apologetics, but it is really better understood than it understands itself, namely on the basis of the Gospel, and in the light of Christ.[2]

2. *Letters and Papers from Prison* (New York, 1953), p. 200.

The fact is that there are many things we do not know about Jesus, for the testimony of the future, and the testimony of other cultures, all of which were made in his image, are not yet in. Christianity does not possess Jesus; it has only begun to comprehend the inexhaustible riches of the Word. It knows Jesus chiefly from the point of view of the white, European races of the past short 2,000 years—a mere fragment of history, a mere fragment of the human race.

4.

If we can learn about Jesus anywhere in history and if grace is everywhere, what advantage is it to be a Christian? To become or remain a Christian because of advantages of which to boast is not, perhaps, wholly admirable. The arrogance of those who possess "good news" withheld from others has not gone unnoticed among the others. To be a Christian has often been dangerous business—has often impaired a man's sense of ignorance, modesty and truthfulness.

To be a Christian is to be a member of a historical people. This people desires to be completely human, but is not yet so. Until now, it represents only a portion of the experience of the human race, only a few cultural traditions and orientations, only a small number of strands of human development. God humbled himself, nevertheless, to speak his inexhaustible Word among this limited people. Thereby he prodded them to expand their inner horizons and to grow in pluralism and diversity, so as to grow up into the stature of Christ, who is all in all. He has prodded them both from within and from without: by the concentrated power of the Word within and by the diffuse riches of the Word without.

The Christian people make their twisting pilgrimage through history in response to the Word revealed to them and nourished among them, and in response to the Word present in

119

every moment of history. Sometimes this people draws reasons for growth from reflection upon its holy books, launching prophetic criticism against the culture in which it finds itself. Sometimes this people draws reasons for growth from the experience of the culture around it, learning to read its own holy books from a new vantage point and in a new way.

To be a Christian is to stand within this people and to benefit by its tradition, its liturgy, its symbols, its wisdom and its fellowship. But to stand within this people as if the goal of the community were to glorify itself, or to establish limits for human development, would be to betray the Word. Creation must not be subordinated to redemption. The world must not be subordinated to the church. The Word is already present in creation, already present in the world. Christians do not "bring" Jesus to the world; he is already there. They go to speak to the world, the relationship is dialogical, and they announce the Word truthfully only if they listen for the presence of the Word already there: abyss cries out to abyss. The missionary enterprise ought not to be a venture in modestly disguised arrogance; it ought to be a venture of discovery.

It is true, of course, that one should not be too optimistic in one's expectations of the world: the Light shone in darkness, and the darkness did not receive it. Yet that same darkness is not outside the church. It is, like the plague of which Camus wrote, in all of us. No one's eye is sound, such that he is inwardly full of light. The struggle between light and darkness, the struggle for even a rudimentary honesty, goes on in each of us.

The purpose of a Christian life is not to become more Christian but less so; not to become more parochial and special but less so. The purpose of a Christian life is to become all that a human being can become, to become more fully human. Man was made in the image of the Word, and through the birth, death and resurrection of Jesus yet more wonderfully restored in that same image. The outermost bounds of that image have never been explored. We do not yet know what it is that Christians, like other men, are capable of becoming. The old cocoons must give way to fresh life in every historical epoch. We are not yet human beings, only striving to become so.

8. Mysticism and Politics

An Epilogue

The revolution is political. But it is, even more, a revolution in consciousness. Through consciousness the question of what is real arises. For most Americans, those things are considered real which are effective, pragmatic, ordered, institutional, scientifically known, conceptually analyzed. Vagrant impulses, fantasies, images, a fundamental wildness and polymorphousness, leaderlessness, purposelessness: such things are taken to be indulgence, unreality, chaos, and nihilism. In order to decide what is to count as real, need we any longer accept the criteria of rationalism? or the criteria of the Protestant ethic, in order to decide what is good? How to make such decisions is now an open question. Hence the dizziness. What is real? In the conflict and confusion, misunderstandings multiply, destructive passions are loosed. The moorings slip. Many of the older generation, once proud of their rationality, barely now control their rage. Many of the younger generation flirt with madness. The ancient issue between being and non-being seems today a struggle between compromise and mad lucidity, between normalcy and insanity. What is real? Even the most solid institutions seem to function like dreams, not for efficiency or for any obvious manifest purpose, but as rituals that fend off darkness and chaos. Churchmen are unreligious, teachers do not teach, corporations are immensely wasteful, the columns of The Wall Street Journal *give the lie to its editorials—nothing is as it seems, or as its rhetoric describes.*

*The young are prone to greet the recurrence of such aware-
ness with the cry "Hypocrisy!" Whereas the nothingness underlying human life is so almost palpable that one wonders:
Do they truly expect honesty? Men cannot bear too much
reality. The truth about our lives induces terror. The young
seem to believe that love, justice, peace, community can be
brought into being, against the void. They have sharp rinsing
feelings and they protect tiny white-hot flames in their chest
(as though these were reasons for hope). Many cannot abide
malice, greed, boredom, flagrant falsehood, complacency.
Many others cannot tolerate evil in themselves. They live in
dread of self-betrayal, tortured by the fear of selling out. The
unspoken truth of the radical young is that the taste of nothingness sits on the bottom of their stomachs, and they need
the theatre of the streets to tear their eyes away.*

*It would not be honest to write of the young as if all were
well with them. In the general faddishness of American life,
it is all too likely that some still newer movement merely
awaits fresh scenes, actors, and rolling news comeras. Yet the
issues identified by the new left, and the battles they began,
cannot afford to be neglected. Whatever happens to the new
left, those battles must be fought. One wishes, therefore, to
criticize the revolution in order to keep it strong; to keep alive
the genuine issues, whichever way public fads and fancies go.*

*In too many ways, the less perceptive, less serious young
merely repeat the values and interests of their parents, under
the guise of a radical rhetoric. In the name of educational
reform, too many substitute grooving in the grass, looking
deeply into each other's eyes, and "honesty" for serious
reading, probing, and critical appreciation. They thus repeat
in eccentric form the anti-intellectualism, the bridge, the
golf, the fraternal organizations, the "frank" good-fellowship
of their parents' generation. Many are not fully alive except
when intoxicated by the sense of fragile danger. They love
to confront the forces of law and order not for strategic gain*

but in order to reply, with too keen a fidelity, the all-too-American scenes of "High Noon": hands non-chalantly near the hip, they amble toward the simple blinding showdown. Conservative editorialists who heap scorn on public administrators for failing "to face up to" student demonstrators comprehend exactly the confrontation politics of many demonstrators: the Goldwater syndrome.

Moreover, there is moral pretension and class snobbery in the purity which many of the young try to maintain in themselves. The cops they so abhor (and sometimes their own parents) were not brought up in a generation that teethed on television, travel, easy money, and intensive schooling. The young may represent a significant new interest group, and their interests may be worth supporting. But it is a mistake to think of them as the bearers of God's truth of moral wisdom, the darlings of nature, history, or manifest destiny. Those who supported Prohibition also thought themselves especially pure. Self-righteousness is a deeply rooted American form, entrapping many who think they have avoided it, when they have merely changed its content. And with self-righteousness, sectarianism, and utopianism. Watch a meeting of radical students —egalitarianism, an open microphone, shouts of approval and disapproval, community songs, clapping hands, swaying bodies, individuals suddenly moved to rush to seize the microphone to voice personal testimony (tears in their eyes)—America has seen this kind of meeting before, often before: these prayer meetings under the open sky, beneath the swaying leaves, where poverty and dirt and freshness rise in the air.

Sincerity and honesty and authenticity are sophisticated ideals, more easily served in word and aspiration than in reality. Freedom is more readily boasted of than attained. (Who in America would admit to not being free?) Emotions are, as guides, as misleading as reason. "All things human, given enough time," a wise old Jesuit used to say, "go badly." We cannot expect the new left to maintain its early goals and fervor. And it is idle to curse the condition that consti-

tutes men political animals. We cannot merely fold our hands and slide into the void. We must enter the world of shadows and struggle amongst what in the end are dreams: build parties, create organizations, devise and direct institutions. Such rituals satisfy neither our wants nor our critical faculties. The towering thirst in us, the terror, is not easily slaked. Everything begins in mysticism, and ends in politics— only to begin again.

The pragmatic commentator and the realistic politician seem, on first glance, to be wary of mysticism. But listen for the echoes of their values: reason, coolness, calculation, measure, efficiency. What could be more mystical? Vietnam is a sample of efficiency? Or the war on poverty? Or General Motors? Or a major university? "Issues are complicated, the capacities of reason are fragile, and we shall at best muddle through in some pragmatic manner." Even the most modest pragmatism is employed by the powers that be; even it cannot disguise its mysticism: belief in glacial amelioration, the ecstasy of hard-headedness.

Angels, perhaps, are mystics through-and-through; men must pass through politics. In two short years, how many events have leapt from the void to slap fear and wonder into us: murders, resignations, astonishing hopes, sadnesses. What does the future hold? One main task of ours is to overcome our class prejudice, to come to sympathetic understanding with the lower middle classes, with firemen, gas station attendants, meter men. These are the most neglected Americans, scorned by the intellectuals, patronized by the mass media, frightened of the rising blacks and the unemployed. It cannot be that such men are inhuman; and in proportion as they are men of flesh, with affections and terrors and loneliness and hopes, they are our teachers. We do not need to despise them, nor to fear them. Nor do they need to be afraid of us. We will have to look for men of politics, and for political parties, that can speak to them as well as to ourselves.

The debts of many decades are coming due: for generations

of slavery and psychological repression wreaked upon the black man; for a welfare state that benefits chiefly the upper and the middle classes—offering federal handouts for highways, airports, harbors, military installations, space and electronics industries, major universities, and new suburban schools; for an educational system geared to the needs of a technological system; for an economic system based, not on the public good, but on profit; for generations cultivating images of simple manly toughness, violence, and brute mastery over a continent.

Brothers and dreamers, there is reason to take heart! A new mysticism becomes, one day, a new politics. Meantime, much suffering must be endured. Later, a yet new mysticism will be required. Politics and mysticism, mysticism and politics.

Be wily as serpents, innocent as robins.

A revolution is a long-term affair. Miracles are not often granted, dreams are smashed, the ghosts of repression sweep broodingly across the land. A revolution requires long marches, defeats, dry seasons. Most of the work is not romantic. A revolution consists in struggling to be free; wrestling with one's personal demons; learning how to understand; beginning to hear—really to hear—the voices of others; breaking the grip of one's own perceptual and imaginative structure[1]; discovering that one can cross racial and class lines without a secret terror; exploring one's sexuality; mastering a trade, a craft, a skill; studying the shape and workings of institutions, and gaining control over them; resisting the daily seduction to treat oneself and others as machines, as means, as parts of the whole ticking, ticking apparatus of a wristwatch-driven nightmare of pure, abstract efficiency; refusing to sell oneself for less than excellence. The work is grubby, inconsequential, endless: revolution is an art. Like a rich art, it has many moods and many themes. It permits—it demands—invention. It is not

1. See R. D. Laing, *The Politics of Experience* (New York, 1967).

an excuse for cutting intelligence short, but for stirring it from a too-habitual sleep.

I began this book as politics. I end it differently. The outline of it grew when I was asked to give the DeYoung Lectures at the University of Southern Illinois in the spring of 1967; the first three chapters derive from those three lectures, which were first published by the Journal *of the University of Southern Illinois, and later in modified form in* The Center Magazine *and finally, in part, in* Motive. *The long fourth chapter from the original outline never found a home. The fifth went to* The Commonweal, *the sixth to* Religion in Life, *and seventh first to* Chr. Kaiser Verlag *in Germany and then to* The Christian Century. *The introduction is adapted from an address to the Honors Convocation at San Jose College in May 1968. Two other intended chapters, "The Revolution of 1976" and "What is Theology's Standpoint?", although they found homes in* The Commonweal *and in* Theology Today, *seemed in the final re-writing to support the main argument of this book too tangentially.*

Our hopes have moved swiftly, often changing forms, in these last two years. So many persons do not understand. Are they from another planet, or are we? Cab drivers, policemen, P.T.A. mothers, Elks, Lions, Rotarians, people in the pews? Is it possible that George Wallace speaks more clearly to America—ten millon Americans—than we? That Richard Nixon is the accurate reflection of our nation? Eli, Eli, lama sabacthani!

The task is clearer now. Many Americans feel forgotten. Many are afraid. We must reach all the people. We do not intend to exclude. How could we—along class lines? or educational lines? geographical lines? religious lines? The revolution cannot be exclusive. Nor can it be victorious. We are not obliged to succeed but to labor.

It is idle to curse the human condition. It is stupid to be alienated from everyone and also from oneself. The exit is to

127

begin—one must begin for oneself, with no one else to say why or how; one must lift oneself by one's ow bootstraps, in an act of gratuitous, creative freedom; one must create oneself out of nothingness. The exit is to begin to experience, to understand, to judge, to decide. For such acts, more than any others, enlarge the range of one's self and of one's world. One must begin (with a little help from one's friends) to feel, to intuit, to evaluate, to do.

The revolution is in the human spirit or not at all.